Oxford School Shakespeare

Othello

edited by
Roma Gill, OBE
M.A. *Cantab*., B.Litt. *Oxon*

Oxford University Press

Oxford   Toronto   Melbourne

Oxford University Press, Great Clarendon Street, Oxford OX2 6DP

Oxford   New York
Athens   Auckland   Bangkok   Bogota   Bombay
Buenos Aires   Calcutta   Cape Town   Dar es Salaam   Delhi
Florence   Hong Kong   Istanbul   Karachi
Kuala Lumpur   Madras   Madrid   Melbourne
Mexico City   Nairobi   Paris   Singapore
Taipei   Tokyo   Toronto   Warsaw

and associated companies in
Berlin   Ibadan

Oxford is a trade mark of Oxford University Press

© Oxford University Press 1989
First published 1989
Reprinted 1991, 1992
This revised edition first published 1993
Reprinted 1994 (twice), 1995, 1996, 1997 (twice)
Trade edition first published 1996
Reprinted 1997 (twice)

ISBN 0 19 831978 9 (School edition)   3 5 7 9 10 8 6 4 2
ISBN 0 19 831995 9 (Trade edition)   3 5 7 9 10 8 6 4 2

Illustrations by Robert Kettell

Cover picture from Primetime shows Willard White in the title role in the television version of the Royal Shakespeare Company's 1989 production of *Othello*.

For Hazel

Printed in Great Britain at the University Press, Cambridge

Contents

Introduction

> It happened that a virtuous lady of wondrous beauty called Disdemona, impelled not by female appetite but by the Moor's good qualities, fell in love with him, and he, vanquished by the Lady's beauty and noble mind, likewise was enamoured of her.

This was the seed from which *Othello* sprang. The passage comes from an Italian collection of stories, Giraldi Cinthio's *Hecatommithi*, which Shakespeare (and many other English dramatists) were reading at the beginning of the seventeenth century. Shakespeare found his plot, and suggestions for his characters, in Cinthio's narrative, whilst both the Italian and the French versions—there seems to have been no English translation at the time—could have provided a few verbal hints for the play. The work was well researched: Shakespeare did not confine himself to a single source. Although he took most from Cinthio, he also borrowed details from a French novelist, Belleforest, and background material from various history books—one of which, Richard Knolle's *General History of the Turks* (published in 1603) provided the name of the mysterious 'Signor Angelo' who is mentioned at 1,3,16 but who is never seen or heard of again.

The play was performed at court in the year 1604; later there were public performances at the Globe Theatre. But *Othello* was not published until 1622; Shakespeare intended his plays to be acted, and there is nothing to suggest that he wanted to see them in print. For many of his plays the only text we have is that of the Folio edition, which was published in 1623 when the plays had been collected together and edited by a couple of the actors who belonged to the company—the King's Men—to which Shakespeare belonged. The first printed text of *Othello*—the quarto edition of 1622, which is referred to as Q1—is not exactly the same as the text printed in the Folio (F). There are some lines in F which are not to be found in Q1, and many of the oaths in Q1 are omitted or modified in F. A modern editor must make use of both editions in preparing a text, relying on judgement and experience to choose between two different readings. This edition is based on F, but adopts a number of Q1 readings, occasionally drawing these to the attention of the reader where they are particularly interesting.

The Place

The first Act of the play takes place in Venice, which in the sixteenth century was a powerful city-state, important to Europe as a commercial centre and to the whole of Christendom as protector of the Christian faith against the Turkish infidels. There are little hints in the first Act of the play which give the impression that Venetian society is orderly, law-abiding, and formal: Brabantio appeals to recognized standards of conduct when he angrily confronts Othello in the presence of the Duke. Cyprus, the setting for the rest of the play, is far less secure. The island had belonged to Venice for more than a hundred years when, about 1570, the Turks began to attack it. The Turkish invasion of Cyprus led to the famous sea-battle of Lepanto in 1571; and although Shakespeare's play was written thirty years after this, his courtly audience in 1604 would have been recently reminded of the battle by a poem on the subject written by their new monarch, James I. Shakespeare uses the Turkish threat (which is not mentioned in Cinthio's story) as a mere pretext; it is useful for removing the play's action to Cyprus (and at the same time demonstrating Othello's importance to Venice). Once Othello and Desdemona have braved the tempestuous seas, they find enough danger on the island.

The People

OTHELLO is a black man in a white society, and a soldier among civilians; he is also one of the greatest lovers in the world's literature.

We learn none of this from the earliest discussion between Iago and Roderigo when they abuse the hated 'Moor', with his 'pride' and his 'thick lips'; later they liken him to 'an old black ram'. So it is a surprise when the Moor appears, in company with Iago whose baseness is immediately revealed when he starts to slander the man who seemed to be his friend. Othello speaks few words at first, and then—with modesty and self-restraint—delivers a speech which, with amazing economy, tells us who and what he is. Othello is a prince, who has done service to the state as the general in command of the military power—it was not unusual for the Venetians to employ foreigners to lead their armies. Othello is confident of his merit, and of his love for 'the gentle Desdemona'. When he is urged to hide from the outraged father, he refuses to run away; he feels secure in the rightness of his position:

> My parts, my title, and my perfect soul
> Shall manifest me rightly.

When he seems to be threatened by the armed Brabantio and his officers, Othello is calm and relaxed enough to ease the tense situation with a quiet joke:

> Keep up your bright swords, for the dew will rust them.

When Brabantio demands an arrest, and it looks as though fighting will break out between the officers and those who support Othello, the Moor keeps the peace with gentle dignity:

> Hold your hands,
> Both you of my inclining and the rest.
> Were it my cue to fight, I should have known it
> Without a prompter.

A magnificent character is being created before our eyes. More—much more—is revealed when Othello defends himself before the Duke. He is respectful to the senators, and begins by telling the truth:

> That I have ta'en away this old man's daughter,
> It is most true; true I have married her.

As he expands his defence, we become increasingly, and *approvingly*, aware of the difference between Othello and the Venetians. Othello does not speak like the rest of the characters: 'Rude am I in my speech' is Othello's description of his own language—but he does not refer to the kind of crude vulgarity which he only learns from Iago as he falls into the ancient's power. Othello does not waste words in polite circumlocutions (unlike the senators who have been speaking before him), and his meaning is never in doubt. His speech has a peculiar magnificence, which is achieved partly through the rhythms and partly by the economic use of a precise and powerful vocabulary. It is displayed at its most eloquent in the description of his 'whole course of love', and the Duke's response to this eloquence must surely speak for all hearers: 'I think this tale would win my daughter too'. Othello, we feel, has *lived*; and Desdemona is to be applauded for her choice of husband.

Love is something new to Othello, and his reaction to Desdemona has a mature intensity that is almost frightening in its richness. As he tells his story to the Duke we can, in the space of some forty lines, watch the development of this mutual feeling from its earliest days, when a shy Desdemona hovered near her father's exciting guest, to its full flowering in the declaration

> She loved me for the dangers I had passed,
> And I loved her, that she did pity them.

The meeting in Cyprus, when Othello is re-united with Desdemona after a perilous voyage, has a sublime happiness which even Othello finds hard to describe: the bliss of heaven cannot equal it. His love has embraced Desdemona, and the two seem to be separate from the rest of the play's characters, in their own world of innocent, joyful loving.

But this earthly paradise has its serpent, and we can never forget the presence of Iago. Only we—the audience—can see his machinations. Every one of the other characters is duped by this 'honest' exterior; and, like them, Othello too is deceived by the man whom he knows and trusts. His belief in Iago is quite understandable: after all, he has worked with him for many years, and must have shared the hardships of battle with him. And although Othello has done the state some service, he is still a foreigner in Venice who does not know the customs of the country, whereas Iago is a Venetian, who seems to be wise in the ways of the world and tells his general: 'I know our country disposition well' (3,3,199). Othello is 'not easily provoked' into jealousy, but when Iago starts his subtle insinuations it is only too easy for Othello to identify *in himself* the possible reasons that could cause Desdemona's love to waver. Chief of these is his colour: 'Haply, for I am black'.

The early scenes of the play emphasized Othello's colour when Iago and Roderigo abused the 'thick lips', and when Brabantio was revolted at the thought of the 'sooty bosom'. But Desdemona 'saw Othello's visage in his mind', and the Duke shared her perception when he told the angry Brabantio that his 'son-in-law [was] far more fair than black'. But since then, the matter of colour has been largely forgotten as Othello was called upon to demonstrate his public authority and his private love. On stage, of course, the reminder is permanently present in the Moor's person: but it has seemed irrelevant. Now it matters intensely: it is Othello's first thought.

But soon the fact of his blackness is forgotten as Othello wrestles with himself, torn between his great love for Desdemona and the doubts, inculcated by Iago, of her faithfulness. Because his love is so great, surpassing all other cares and affections, the thought of its betrayal is equally overwhelming: there is no longer purpose anywhere—'Othello's occupation's gone' (3,3,354). His threats to Iago, promising not physical pain but eternal damnation, have a heated violence which is frightening to read—and contrast with the cold, measured lines in which he declares his resolution, comparing himself to the sea 'Whose icy current and compulsive course Ne'er feels retiring ebb, but keeps due on'.

Yet this declaration, however, is not final. Othello must experience more anguish, caused in the first place by Iago's calculated slander.

The mental suffering is expressed physically when he falls to the ground in passion: even his body is no longer under his control, almost as though he were experiencing some kind of diabolic possession. Iago dismisses the frenzy as a commonplace epileptic seizure—'his second fit; he had one yesterday'. The excuse may satisfy Cassio—or at least have the desired effect of sending him away from the scene—but it is not an adequate explanation for Othello's distress. There is nothing usual about this episode: Othello's sense of wrong, like his feeling for Desdemona, is of heroic dimensions.

His subsequent conduct towards Desdemona, however, is less than heroic. Having been confronted with Iago's 'ocular proof'—the missing handkerchief—the Moor treats his wife as though she were a loathed prostitute. The powerful love turns to almighty hatred of the supposed deed of adultery rather than the woman herself, for it is the deed which has defeated his highest ideals.

When, at the beginning of the last scene, Othello approaches Desdemona's bed, we see that his love is by no means extinguished. He reacts with acute sensitivity to her warm, sleeping, beauty which he experiences as physically as the scent of a rose—the most potent of all English flowers. This speech and the death of Desdemona must surely make the most beautiful of all literary murder scenes! But when his wife lies at peace, Othello must experience the most cruel torture he has so far endured. Emilia, Iago's wife, reveals the truth of the situation, and Othello is the most miserable of men. A deeply religious man, he looks at the murdered body and foresees his own punishment—he will be condemned on the Day of Judgement to eternal damnation:

> When we shall meet at compt
> This look of thine will hurl my soul from heaven
> And fiends will snatch at it.

When the Venetians, Gratiano and Lodovico, begin the process of 'tidying up', Othello is quiet, submissive, and repentant. He is arrested, but before he can be removed from the scene he interrupts with a speech that restores his heroic stature and—with a sudden, unexpected, stroke—rescues his nobility. Othello becomes one of Shakespeare's great tragic heroes.

DESDEMONA should have made a most successful marriage—in the eyes of Venetian society. She belonged to one of the city's noblest families, and could have been the bride of any one of its most eligible bachelors—'the wealthy curled darlings of our nation'. A girl 'so tender, fair, and happy', accustomed to coping with 'the house affairs' for her father, would have made a good wife for any man. She is also sexually attractive (as well as beautiful): all the men who speak of her refer to her ability to arouse them—and even Iago flirts with her.

But Desdemona has a mind of her own. In the past, before the play opened, she had refused to marry, being 'opposite to marriage' and rejecting the husbands of her father's choice. Now she has met, loved, and married the man of her own heart: she has given herself, body and soul, to Othello—the black man. Her father thought she must be out of her mind, driven to such a mad action by drugs or even witchcraft; but the only magical power used by Othello is his own personal magnetism, which drew Desdemona from the dreary household chores to learn about a world of adventure and excitement from a man of courage and daring. The colour of his skin did not matter: Desdemona 'saw Othello's visage in his mind', and gave up everything—her father's love, her fortune, and her reputation in the polite society of Venice—to love and live with him.

This is a woman to equal Othello's bravery. As the play unfolds, the different aspects of Desdemona's character are revealed, and blend into a unique personality. Her independence asserts itself again when she refuses to stay in her father's house whilst Othello is away, and begs leave to accompany her soldier husband to the garrison island of Cyprus. She states a magnificently erotic commitment to Othello:

> My heart's subdued
> Even to the utmost pleasure of my lord.

When Desdemona arrives in Cyprus, we become conscious of another attribute: we already know of her birth, beauty, intelligence, and love—but now Cassio's remarks add a new dimension. He calls her 'divine', and although this may seem the sort of hyperbole that is typical of such a courtier, we can recognize something other in his greeting:

> Hail to thee, lady! And the grace of heaven,
> Before, behind thee, and on every hand,
> Enwheel thee round.

The quality—grace—which he wishes for Desdemona is difficult to explain, but it characterizes all her conduct, whether active—in the things she does—or passive, in her suffering. Shakespeare's concept of 'grace' is a Christian one: theologically it is defined as the supernatural assistance given by God for the sanctification of the human being.

For a moment the action of the play seems to stand still; then, as Desdemona accepts Cassio's blessing with thanks, the business begins again and an anxious wife waits to be reunited with her husband. A lesser person might have shown her anxiety to those around—but Othello's wife must keep her feelings hidden, confiding only in the audience:

> I am not merry, but I do beguile
> The thing I am by seeming otherwise.

And once the two are together again, she looks forward to a life of ever-increasing love and happiness.

This, of course, is not to be. Desdemona pleads for Cassio with a fervour that could only come from innocence; she cannot imagine that any interpretation, other than her intended meaning, could be put upon her words. To suggest that she is being tactless when she persists in her efforts is to reveal our own sophistication! She bears Othello's abuse with meekness and patience, allowing only a brief expression of bewildered bitterness, and never swerving in her love for her husband. The outraged Emilia utters the words that any woman might speak, 'I would you had never seen him', but Desdemona is firm: 'So would not I'. And her dying words, after declaring her death to be 'guiltless', are an attempt to divert the blame away from Othello by taking it upon herself and speaking a last goodbye: 'Commend me to my kind lord. O farewell'.

EMILIA is in some ways the foil to her mistress, setting off Desdemona's spiritual beauty by contrast with her earthy commonsense. This is achieved particularly in the quiet scene (*Act 4*, Scene 3) when she talks to Desdemona about women and their husbands. If Desdemona is listening, she does not appear to comprehend Emilia's easy, witty, answers to her troubled questioning. But even the worldly-wise Emilia is blind to her husband's wickedness. She describes, most aptly, the 'eternal villain' who has slandered Desdemona; but she fails to identify him.

Iago's wife, although he abuses her with a rough good humour, has some loyalty and obedience to her 'wayward husband'—enough to pick up Desdemona's handkerchief and give it to him, without knowing why he wants it. But even Emilia, when she learns the truth of Desdemona's death, reaches towards heroic stature.

IAGO himself, however, is a very different character from all the others in the play. He *seems* to be a friend to all—Othello's trusted 'ancient', Roderigo's ally, counsellor to the downcast Cassio, even adviser to the wretched Desdemona when she has lost her husband's favour. Most praise him as 'honest Iago'; but only to the audience does he show anything of his real self. The rest of the characters have only partial glimpses—and even the audience must make its own judgement on some of the reasons offered by Iago to explain his actions.

He tells Roderigo that he hates the Moor because Othello has chosen another man, Cassio, as his second-in-command, preferring him above Iago. This seems to be the chief motive for his vindictiveness. His anger is that of a man who has been rejected and despised, whose service and experience have been down-graded, and whose career is blocked for lack of paper qualifications. It is, one recognizes, an understandable reaction; but it provokes revenge out of all proportion.

Another motive follows fast upon the exposition of this reasonable disappointment, but this one is wholly irrational: Iago hates Othello because he is black. In the presence of his general, Iago appears loyal and respectful: behind Othello's back he loses no opportunity to abuse or diminish him. This is the reaction of one who, because he feels himself to be inferior, tries to reduce everyone to his own level.

Frequently in conversation Iago shows this 'reductive' tendency, sneering at Roderigo's passions, abusing women—even the most beautiful and virtuous are good only 'To suckle fools, and chronicle small beer'—and casting doubt on the integrity and competence of his superiors (slandering Cassio for drunkenness, and suggesting that Othello is a regular abuser of his wife).

But nothing describes Iago so well as his own observation when, referring to Cassio, he remarks

> He hath a daily beauty in his life
> That makes me ugly.

And Iago *is* ugly; in the proverbial saying, he is 'ugly as sin'. The notion that white/black = good/evil is confounded in Iago, than whom no one could be more opposed to Othello.

BRABANTIO is Desdemona's father, and a member of the Venetian senate. He is outraged when his daughter makes a secret marriage with a black man.

RODERIGO is a young Venetian nobleman who believes himself to be in love with Desdemona. Brabantio refuses to accept him as a suitor for his daughter, but he has been duped by Iago into sending many gifts to Desdemona (which, of course, Iago has kept for himself).

CASSIO, Othello's lieutenant, serves in the Venetian army, although he is a native of Florence. Through Iago's machinations, he becomes involved in a fight, loses his position, and appeals to Desdemona to get him reinstated in Othello's favour.

The Action

Act 1

Scene 1   Roderigo and Iago inform Brabantio of Desdemona's secret marriage to Othello. Enraged, Brabantio sets out in search of his daughter.

Scene 2   Iago warns Othello that Brabantio is searching for him. Cassio brings a summons from the Duke demanding Othello's presence at court on a matter of urgent state business. Brabantio accuses Othello of abducting Desdemona, and orders him to be arrested. But the Duke's command must be answered first.

Scene 3   The Duke is hearing about the threatened Turkish invasion of Cyprus, and he welcomes the arrival of Othello and Brabantio. He hears Brabantio's accusation and Othello's defence, sending for Desdemona to testify to her love. The Duke tries to pacify Brabantio, and then turns his attention to the Turkish threat. He orders Othello to go to Cyprus. Othello welcomes the command, and Desdemona requests permission to go with her husband. Her request is granted. Roderigo now despairs of ever winning Desdemona's love, but Iago has a scheme that excites fresh hope in him. Roderigo prepares to sail to Cyprus, and Iago speaks his thoughts aloud.

Act 2

Scene 1   In Cyprus, Othello's arrival is anxiously awaited, although the Turkish fleet is no longer a threat. Cassio's ship has docked, then Desdemona arrives, accompanied by Iago. He makes jokes until she is safely reunited with Othello. Iago suggests to Roderigo that Desdemona is in love with Cassio. Left alone on the stage, Iago once again speaks his thoughts aloud.

Scene 2   The Herald proclaims that there will be free drinks for all, in celebration of Othello's marriage.

Scene 3   Iago has got Roderigo drunk, and he now persuades Cassio to drink too much. A quarrel is started, in which Cassio strikes Roderigo. Iago sounds the alarm, bringing Othello on to the scene. When Othello hears Iago's account of the fighting, he immediately dismisses Cassio from his office as lieutenant. Othello retires with Desdemona. Cassio grieves over the loss of his position, but Iago comforts him by suggesting that Desdemona will plead with Othello to have him reinstated. Alone on stage, Iago outlines his plan of action, and then he assures Roderigo that everything is under control.

Act 3

Scene 1   Cassio brings musicians to serenade Desdemona. He asks Emilia (who has been sent out by Iago) to let him see her mistress.

Scene 2   Othello leaves his quarters, and goes to inspect the island's fortifications.

Scene 3   Desdemona promises Cassio that she will intercede for him. Othello returns with Iago. Desdemona pleads for Cassio, and Othello is not unsympathetic. But when Desdemona has gone, Iago begins his insinuations. He causes Othello to doubt Desdemona and her friendship with Cassio. Desdemona comes to call Othello for dinner, and as she leaves the stage—with her husband—she drops her hand-kerchief. Emilia picks it up and gives it to Iago. When Othello returns to the scene, he is already very jealous. Iago fans his suspicions, claiming to have seen Desdemona's handkerchief in Cassio's hands. Othello swears that he will be revenged, and orders Iago to kill Cassio.

Scene 4   Othello asks Desdemona for the handkerchief that she has lost, but she tries to talk to him about Cassio. Othello leaves in a rage. When Cassio comes in, with Iago, Desdemona tells them that her husband is behaving strangely—and Iago goes after Othello. Emilia suggests that Othello may be jealous, but Desdemona declares that he has absolutely no cause for jealousy. As the two women leave, Bianca comes in search of Cassio. He shows her a handkerchief that he has found in his room, and asks Bianca to copy its embroidery.

Act 4

Scene 1   Iago persists in his insinuations until Othello, anguished at the thought that Desdemona might be unfaithful to him, falls into an epileptic convulsion. When he recovers consciousness, Iago promises to get proof of what he has been saying. Othello conceals himself, and listens whilst Iago and Cassio talk about a woman. He assumes that they are discussing Desdemona, and is now convinced of her guilt. Letters recalling Othello to Venice are brought by Lodovico; Othello strikes and insults his wife in the presence of this messenger.

Scene 2   Othello questions Emilia about his wife's conduct. He sends for Desdemona, and accuses her of adultery. She is very distressed. Emilia tries to comfort her, then goes to fetch her own husband. Iago speaks some words of comfort to Desdemona—and then proceeds with his own schemes, setting up Roderigo to attack (and try to kill) Cassio.

Scene 3   Whilst Desdemona is preparing for bed, she talks to Emilia about unfaithful wives.

Act 5

Scene 1   Roderigo (instructed by Iago) lies in wait for Cassio as he comes from Bianca's house. There is a quick skirmish of fighting, in which both Roderigo and Cassio are wounded. The cries arouse Othello, who assumes that Iago has murdered Cassio (as he had promised to do in *Act 3*, Scene 3). Lodovico and Gratiano hasten to see what is the matter, and Iago also appears on the scene. He takes control of the situation, sending Emilia back to Othello and Desdemona.

Scene 2   Othello comes to Desdemona in her bed-chamber, determined to kill her. He accuses her of having committed adultery with Cassio and, although Desdemona pleads her innocence, he covers her head with a pillow and suffocates her. Emilia brings news of the fighting and the death of Roderigo. When she sees the murdered Desdemona, and hears Othello's accusation, she raises the alarm; this fetches Iago, Gratiano, and Montano into the room. Emilia denounces Iago, who draws his sword on her and escapes from the scene. He is brought back, however, with Cassio; and the full truth is revealed. Othello, convinced of his own guilt, stabs himself. Iago is arrested and taken away to be tortured.

Time Sequences in *Othello*

On the stage *Othello* moves very fast—a great swirl of activity which is physical, mental, and above all emotional. Quarrels are struck up, hatreds develop, and love flowers into death. How long does all this take? In the theatre we are too involved—excited, delighted, frightened, and saddened—to worry about little matters of 'when' and 'how long'. Reading is a slower business, allowing us leisure to ask how, for example, could Desdemona and Cassio have the opportunity for adultery, since they sailed from Venice (in separate ships) on the day after the marriage with Othello had been revealed, and seem to have spent only a short time—minutes, perhaps hours—in Cyprus before the arrival of the Moor.

But such questions are irrelevant. When Shakespeare wants us to think about time, as he does in *Act 2*, Scene 3, he gives very clear directions: it 'is not yet ten o'clock' when the scene opens, and early morning when it ends. But when Bianca is berating Cassio for not visiting her, we are meant to be amused at her reproach—not to check her arithmetic:

> What, keep a week away? Seven days and nights?
> Eight score eight hours? And lovers' absent hours
> More tedious than the dial eight score times.

How can Cassio have stayed away from her for so long? How long has he been on the island? Does it matter?

The dramatist's hours are infinitely more *flexible* 'than the dial'; critics speak very learnedly of 'the double time scheme' in *Othello*, but I suspect there is really only one time scheme—Shakespeare's time—which contracts and expands both the clock and the calendar to suit its own needs.

Shakespeare's Verse

Shakespeare's plays are mainly written in 'blank verse', the form preferred by most dramatists in the sixteenth and early seventeenth centuries. It is a very flexible medium, which is capable—like the human speaking voice—of a wide range of tones. Basically the lines, which are unrhymed, are ten syllables long. The syllables have alternating stresses, just like normal English speech; and they divide into five 'feet'. The technical name for this is 'iambic pentameter'.

> And whát was hé?
> Forsóoth, a gréat aríthmetícián,
> One Míchael Cássió, a Flórentíne —
> A féllow álmost dámned in á fair wífe —
> That néver sét a squádron ín the fíeld,
> Nor thé devísion óf a báttle knóws
> More thán a spínster—unléss the bóokish théoríc,
> Whereín the tógèd cónsuls cán propóse
> As másterlý as hé. Mere práttle wíthout práctice
> Is áll his sóldiershíp. But hé, sir, hád th'eléction:
> And Í, of whóm his éyes had séen the próof
> At Rhódes, at Cýprus, ánd on óther gróunds
> Christián and héathen, múst be léed and cálmed
> By débitór and créditór; this cóunter-cáster,
> He iń good tíme must hís lieuténant bé,
> And Í—God bléss the márk—his Móorship's
>   ańciént.
>
> (lines 19–33)

When Iago begins this description of the man who has been preferred before him, the lines are regular—his hatred is controlled. But soon his anger runs away with him; the normal rhythm breaks sometimes under the stress, and additional syllables crowd into the line. The verse line sometimes contains the grammatical unit of meaning—'That never set a squadron in the field'—thus allowing for a pause at the end of the line, before a new idea is started; at other times, the sense runs on from one line to the next—'knows More than a spinster'. This makes for the natural fluidity of speech, avoiding monotony but still maintaining the iambic rhythm.

Characters in the play

Othello   *a Moor, general in the Venetian army*
Desdemona   *his wife*
Cassio   *his lieutenant*
Iago   *his ancient (ensign)*
Emilia   *wife of Iago*
Bianca   *a prostitute, Cassio's mistress*
Roderigo   *a Venetian gentleman in love with Desdemona*
Clown   *servant in Othello's household*

Duke of Venice
Brabantio   *a Venetian senator, Desdemona's father*
Gratiano   *his brother*
Lodovico   *his kinsman*
Montano   *governor of Cyprus*

Herald
Sailor
Messenger

Venetian senators, Gentlemen of Cyprus,
Musicians,
Soldiers, Attendants, and Servants

SCENE: The first Act takes place in Venice; the rest of the play
is set in Cyprus

Act I

Act I   Scene I

At night, in a street outside Brabantio's house in Venice, two men whisper their secret griefs. Roderigo is angry because he believes that Iago has cheated him; and Iago is full of hatred for someone he calls 'the Moor'. They rouse Brabantio from his bed with news of his daughter's rebellion—although Iago deserts Roderigo before the angry father arrives on stage. Brabantio institutes a search for Desdemona.

1   *Tush, never tell me*: 'Rubbish, don't try to make me believe that'; the play opens in the middle of a conversation.

3   *strings*: which fastened the purse; Iago has been using Roderigo's money as though it were his own.

4   *'Sblood*: Iago swears by God's blood; the violent oath is fitting for the soldier.
hear me: listen to me.

8   *great ones*: important men.

9   *In personal suit*: Went to him themselves.
lieutenant: second-in-command.

10 *Off-capped*: Took off their hats (as a sign of respect).

11 *my price*: what I'm worth.

12 *as loving*: preferring.

13 *a bombast circumstance*: some fancy reason (*bombast* was a kind of cotton stuffing, used for padding clothes).

14 *epithets of war*: military jargon.

16 *Non-suits*: Refuses their request.
Certes: To be sure.

19 *Forsooth...arithmetician*: Iago scorns Cassio because he is nothing but an administrator: he understands the theory of warfare, but not the practice.

20 *a Florentine*: In the sixteenth century, Florence was a centre of commerce and banking.

21 *damned in a fair wife*: In the play Cassio is unmarried—but see p.126. Iago seems to be

Scene I

Enter Roderigo *and* Iago

Roderigo
Tush, never tell me! I take it much unkindly
That thou, Iago, who hast had my purse
As if the strings were thine, shouldst know of this.

Iago
'Sblood, but you will not hear me!
5   If ever I did dream of such a matter,
Abhor me.

Roderigo
Thou told'st me thou didst hold him in thy hate.

Iago
Despise me, if I do not. Three great ones of the city,
In personal suit to make me his lieutenant,
10 Off-capped to him: and by the faith of man,
I know my price, I am worth no worse a place.
But he, as loving his own pride and purposes,
Evades them with a bombast circumstance
Horribly stuffed with epithets of war,
15 And in conclusion
Non-suits my mediators. For 'Certes,' says he,
'I have already chose my officer.'
And what was he?
Forsooth, a great arithmetician,
20 One Michael Cassio, a Florentine—
A fellow almost damned in a fair wife—
That never set a squadron in the field,
Nor the devision of a battle knows
More than a spinster—unless the bookish theoric,
25 Wherein the togèd consuls can propose
As masterly as he. Mere prattle without practice
Is all his soldiership. But he, sir, had th'election:

saying that a weakness for women will be the ruin of Cassio—or perhaps his marriage to a pretty woman will ruin him because (in the opinion of a cynic like Iago) all pretty women are false to their husbands.

22 *set...field*: placed a company of soldiers on the battlefield for a 'pitched', or formal, battle (rather than a casual skirmish).

23 *devision*: devising—the strategical placing of soldiers.

24 *a spinster*: someone (usually a woman) whose job is to spin wool.
unless the bookish theoric: except for what he has read in books.

25 *togèd*: wearing a toga—the dress of peace in ancient Rome.
propose: give advice.

27 *had th'election*: got the job.

28 *proof*: proven ability.

30 *leed*: i.e. like a sailing ship that is forced into the calm waters where it cannot find any wind.

31 *debitor and creditor*: a mere book-keeper (one who works out debits and credits).
counter-caster: one who adds sums, using metal counters; Iago continues to think of Cassio as an 'arithmetician'.

33 *God bless the mark*: God help us; an exclamation of impatience.
his Moorship's ancient: his Moorish lordship's ensign (= standard-bearer).

35 *'Tis ... service*: That's the trouble with this job.

36 *Preferment goes by*: Promotion depends on.
letter: academic qualifications.
affection: favouritism.

37 *by old gradation*: according to seniority, as it used to.

39 *in any just term*: in any reasonable way.
affined: bound.

40 *follow him*: serve under his command.

41 *content you*: don't you worry.
serve my turn upon him: use him for my own advantage.

45 *knee-crooking*: bowing, bending his knees.

46 *doting on*: enjoying.

48 *provender*: food and drink.
cashiered: dismissed, sacked.

49 *Whip me*: A contemptuous dismissal.

50 *trimmed ... duty*: showing all outward signs of obedience.

51 *Keep ... themselves*: Think of themselves.

52 *throwing ... lords*: only giving the appearance that they are working for their masters.

And I, of whom his eyes had seen the proof
At Rhodes, at Cyprus, and on other grounds
30 Christian and heathen, must be leed and calmed
By debitor and creditor; this counter-caster,
He in good time must his lieutenant be,
And I—God bless the mark!—his Moorship's ancient.
    Roderigo
By heaven, I rather would have been his hangman.
    Iago
35 Why, there's no remedy. 'Tis the curse of service:
Preferment goes by letter and affection,
And not by old gradation, where each second
Stood heir to th'first. Now sir, be judge yourself
Whether I in any just term am affined
40 To love the Moor.
    Roderigo   I would not follow him then.
    Iago O sir, content you:
I follow him to serve my turn upon him.
We cannot all be masters, nor all masters
Cannot be truly followed. You shall mark
45 Many a duteous and knee-crooking knave
That, doting on his own obsequious bondage,
Wears out his time, much like his master's ass,
For naught but provender, and when he's
    old—cashiered!

53 *well thrive*: succeed.
   lined their coats: made a profit for themselves.
54 *Do ... homage*: Have a good opinion of themselves.
   soul: spirit.
58 *Were ... Iago*: This is a cryptic remark, which sounds very well but means very little.
60 *Heaven ... duty*: Iago claims to be telling the honest truth, that he does not serve Othello for love or out of a sense of duty.
61 *peculiar*: personal.
62 *outward action*: action which can be seen.
63 *native act*: real action.
   figure: nature.
64 *compliment extern*: outward show.
65 *wear ... sleeve*: Serving-men wore badges on the sleeves of their uniforms.
66 *daws*: jackdaws (thought to be very foolish birds); the Folio text has 'doves', which are very mild, gentle birds.
   I am not what I am: I am not what I appear to be.
67 *full*: good.
   the thick-lips: an insulting reference to the man whom Iago calls 'the Moor'—and an indication that he is negroid.
   owe: own.
68 *carry't thus*: get away with it, succeed.
   her father: Desdemona's father, Brabantio.
69 *him*: i.e. Othello.
   make after: follow.
70 *Proclaim him*: Denounce him as a thief.
71-2 *though ... flies*: although he's happy now, let's spoil things for him. The famous 'plague of flies' was sent to the Egyptians who were oppressing the Hebrews and refusing to let them seek out the Promised Land (*Exodus* 8:20).
72 *his joy be joy*: his happiness is true happiness.
73 *throw ... vexation*: suggest such possibilities of trouble.
74 *lose some colour*: fade, become doubtful.
76 *timorous*: frightening.
77 *by night and negligence*: the fire is seen *at* night, and was caused *by* negligence.

81 *bags*: money-bags.

Whip me such honest knaves. Others there are
50 Who, trimmed in forms and visages of duty,
Keep yet their hearts attending on themselves,
And, throwing but shows of service on their lords,
Do well thrive by them; and when they have lined
    their coats,
Do themselves homage: these fellows have some soul,
55 And such a one do I profess myself.
For, sir,
It is as sure as you are Roderigo,
Were I the Moor, I would not be Iago:
In following him, I follow but myself.
60 Heaven is my judge, not I for love and duty,
But seeming so for my peculiar end:
For when my outward action doth demonstrate
The native act and figure of my heart
In compliment extern, 'tis not long after,
65 But I will wear my heart upon my sleeve
For daws to peck at—I am not what I am.
    Roderigo
What a full fortune does the thick-lips owe
If he can carry't thus!
    Iago   Call up her father,
Rouse him, make after him, poison his delight,
70 Proclaim him in the streets, incense her kinsmen;
And, though he in a fertile climate dwell,
Plague him with flies; though that his joy be joy,
Yet throw such chances of vexation on't,
As it may lose some colour.
    Roderigo
75 Here is her father's house; I'll call aloud.
    Iago
Do, with like timorous accent and dire yell,
As when, by night and negligence, the fire
Is spied in populous cities.
    Roderigo
What ho, Brabantio! Signor Brabantio, ho!
    Iago
80 Awake! What ho, Brabantio! Thieves, thieves!
Look to your house, your daughter, and your bags!
Thieves, thieves!

82sd *above*: Some Elizabethan playhouses
    seem to have had a balcony at the back of
    the stage, which could be used here to
    represent the upper floor of Brabantio's
    house.

87 *Zounds*: Iago swears by God's wounds.

90 *tupping*: copulating with (Iago uses the
    language of sheep-farmers).
91 *snorting*: snoring.
92 *the devil*: In some traditions, the devil is
    depicted as black.
    grandsire: grandfather.
94 *Most reverend signor*: Roderigo is extremely
    respectful.
    know my voice: the figures cannot be
    recognized in the dark.

Enter Brabantio *above, at a window*

Brabantio
What is the reason of this terrible summons?
What is the matter there?
Roderigo
85 Signor, is all your family within?
Iago
Are your doors locked?
Brabantio   Why, wherefore ask you this?
Iago
Zounds, sir, you're robbed; for shame, put on your
    gown;
Your heart is burst, you have lost half your soul.
Even now, now, very now, an old black ram
90 Is tupping your white ewe. Arise, arise,
Awake the snorting citizens with the bell,
Or else the devil will make a grandsire of you.
Arise, I say!
Brabantio
                 What, have you lost your wits?
Roderigo
Most reverend signor, do you know my voice?

97 *charged*: ordered.
  haunt about: hang around.
98 *in honest plainness*: plain, straightforward
  language.
99 *for thee*: intended for you to marry.
100 *distempering draughts*: intoxicating drink.
101 *Upon malicious bravery*: With mischievous
  impudence.
102 *start*: disturb.

103 *thou must needs be sure*: you can rest
  assured.
104 *spirit*: courage.
  place: position.

106-7 *This ... grange*: Brabantio's house is not
  some lonely country farm, but is situated in
  a busy city.
108 *In simple and pure soul*: With the most
  honest intentions.
109-10 *you are ... bid you*: i.e. 'you are the
  sort of person who will not take good
  advice because you dislike the man who
  offers it'.
112 *covered with*: mated with.
  Barbary horse: the Barbary coast of North
  Africa was famous for horse-breeding.
113 *coursers*: racehorses.
  cousins: kindred.
114 *jennets*: mules (also small Spanish horses).
  germans: blood relations.
117 *making the beast with two backs*: having
  sexual intercourse.
119 *senator*: The name does not insult
  Brabantio, but the tone in which it is
  uttered must indicate Iago's scorn.
120 *know thee, Roderigo*: Brabantio assumes
  that the abusive language was spoken by
  Roderigo.
121 *answer*: pay for (i.e. insulting him).
122 'If it is with your agreement and
  permission'.
123 *partly*: to some extent (since Brabantio
  seems unconcerned).
124 *odd-even*: after midnight.
  dull: sleepy time.
  watch: division of the night.
126 *common hire*: available for general hire

Brabantio

95 Not I: what are you?

Roderigo   My name is Roderigo.

Brabantio

The worser welcome!
I have charged thee not to haunt about my doors.
In honest plainness thou hast heard me say
My daughter is not for thee. And now in madness,
100 Being full of supper and distempering draughts,
Upon malicious bravery dost thou come
To start my quiet.

Roderigo

Sir, sir, sir—

Brabantio   But thou must needs be sure
My spirit and my place have in them power
105 To make this bitter to thee.

Roderigo   Patience, good sir.

Brabantio

What tell'st thou me of robbing? This is Venice:
My house is not a grange.

Roderigo   Most grave Brabantio,
In simple and pure soul I come to you—

Iago

Zounds, sir, you are one of those that will not serve
110 God if the devil bid you. Because we come to do you
service, and you think we are ruffians, you'll have
your daughter covered with a Barbary horse; you'll
have your nephews neigh to you, you'll have
coursers for cousins, and jennets for germans.

Brabantio

115 What profane wretch art thou?

Iago

I am one, sir, that comes to tell you, your daughter
and the Moor are now making the beast with two
backs.

Brabantio

Thou art a villain.

Iago   You are a senator.

Brabantio

120 This thou shalt answer. I know thee, Roderigo.

Roderigo

Sir, I will answer everything. But I beseech you
If't be your pleasure and most wise consent,

(not the servant of any private family).
127 *clasps*: embraces.
128 *your allowance*: has your consent.
129 *saucy*: insolent.
130 *my manners*: code of conduct.
131 *We have ... rebuke*: You are wrong to
     reproach us.
132 *from ... civility*: contrary to all decent
     behaviour.
133 *trifle with*: treat lightly.
     your reverence: a nobleman like you.
135 *revolt*: rebellion.
136 *Tying ... In*: Trusting ... to.
137 *extravagant*: wandering.
     wheeling: free-ranging.
     stranger: foreigner.
138 *Of here and everywhere*: Who doesn't
     belong anywhere.
     Straight: Immediately.
     satisfy yourself: see for yourself.
141 *Strike on the tinder*: Make a light (i.e. with
     flint and tinder box).
142 *taper*: candle.
143 *This accident*: What has happened.
145 *Farewell*: Iago slips away as soon as there
     is any risk of discovery.
146 *meet*: suitable.
     nor wholesome to my place: not good for
     my job.
147 *produced*: called as a witness.
149 *gall*: hurt.
     check: rebuke.
150 *cast*: dismiss.
151 *embarked*: engaged.
     loud: good.
152 *even now*: at this very moment.
     stand in act: are being fought.
     for their souls: for all that they are worth.
153 *fathom*: ability.
154 *lead their business*: conduct their affairs.
     In which regard: For this reason (i.e. that
     Othello is the best man for the job of
     leading the Venetian forces).

As partly I find it is, that your fair daughter,
At this odd-even and dull watch o'th'night,
125 Transported with no worse nor better guard
But with a knave of common hire, a gondolier,
To the gross clasps of a lascivious Moor—
If this be known to you, and your allowance,
We then have done you bold and saucy wrongs;
130 But if you know not this, my manners tell me
We have your wrong rebuke. Do not believe
That from the sense of all civility
I would thus play and trifle with your reverence.
Your daughter, if you have not given her leave,
135 I say again hath made a gross revolt,
Tying her duty, beauty, wit, and fortunes
In an extravagant and wheeling stranger
Of here and everywhere. Straight satisfy yourself:
If she be in her chamber or your house,
140 Let loose on me the justice of the state
For thus deluding you.
    Brabantio   Strike on the tinder, ho!
Give me a taper; call up all my people!
This accident is not unlike my dream:
Belief of it oppresses me already.
145 Light, I say, light!   [*Exit above*
    Iago   Farewell, for I must leave you.
It seems not meet, nor wholesome to my place,
To be produced—as if I stay, I shall—
Against the Moor. For I do know the state
(However this may gall him with some check)
150 Cannot with safety cast him; for he's embarked
With such loud reason to the Cyprus wars,
Which even now stand in act, that for their souls
Another of his fathom they have none
To lead their business. In which regard,

155 *hell pains*: the torments of hell.
156 *for ... life*: because my living at present depends on it.
157 *show ... love*: give all appearances of loyalty; Iago's metaphor comes appropriately from one who is a standard-bearer.
158 *but sign*: only an appearance.
     That: So that.
     surely: be certain to.
159 *Sagittary*: The Sagittarius, an inn whose sign was that of the armed centaur (half-man, half-horse) in the zodiacal sign.
     raisèd search: the search-party that he must raise.

160sd *night-gown*: dressing-gown.
162–3 *what's ... bitterness*: Brabantio fears that the rest of his life will be nothing but misery, since he will be scorned by society (for having a disobedient daughter).
163 *Now, Roderigo*: Brabantio's attitude to Roderigo is beginning to change.
164 *unhappy*: unfortunate.
167 *Past thought*: More than I could ever have thought.
170 *Treason of the blood*: Desdemona's passion ('blood') has betrayed her reason; *and* Desdemona's rebellion against her father is a betrayal of her family ('blood').
171 *From hence*: From this example.
172 *Is*: Elizabethan grammar permitted the singular form where modern English would demand 'Are'.
173 *property*: nature—i.e. innocence.
174 *May*: Can.
176 *would ... her*: I wish you had married her.
177 *Some ... another*: Brabantio directs the servants to go in different directions.
182 *I may ... most*: Brabantio is an important citizen who has influence over most of the people in Venice, and can get assistance from most families.
183 *special officers of night*: The Venetian State had a special police force for night duties.
184 *I'll ... pains*: I'll reward you for your trouble.

155 Though I do hate him as I do hell pains,
     Yet for necessity of present life
     I must show out a flag and sign of love,
     Which is indeed but sign. That you shall surely find him,
     Lead to the Sagittary the raisèd search;
160 And there will I be with him. So farewell.   [*Exit*

     Enter Brabantio *in his night-gown, and*
     Servants *with torches*

     Brabantio
     It is too true an evil. Gone she is,
     And what's to come of my despisèd time
     Is naught but bitterness. Now, Roderigo,
     Where didst thou see her?—O unhappy girl!—
165 With the Moor, say'st thou?—Who would be a father?—
     How didst thou know 'twas she?—O she deceives me
     Past thought!—What said she to you?—Get more tapers.
     Raise all my kindred.—Are they married, think you?
     Roderigo
     Truly I think they are.
     Brabantio
170 O heaven! How got she out? O treason of the blood!
     Fathers, from hence trust not your daughters' minds
     By what you see them act. Is there not charms
     By which the property of youth and maidhood
     May be abused? Have you not read, Roderigo,
175 Of some such thing?
     Roderigo   Yes, sir, I have indeed.
     Brabantio
     Call up my brother—O would you had had her—
     Some one way, some another. Do you know
     Where we may apprehend her and the Moor?
     Roderigo
     I think I can discover him, if you please
180 To get good guard and go along with me.
     Brabantio
     Pray you, lead on. At every house I'll call—
     I may command at most. Get weapons, ho!
     And raise some special officers of night.
     On, good Roderigo, I'll deserve your pains.   [*Exeunt*

Act I   Scene 2

Iago now presents himself as Othello's friend, willing to defend his honour, and anxious for his safety now that he is married to Desdemona. Othello speaks confidently of his love, but he is interrupted by the approach of a search party—Cassio is seeking Othello on the Duke's orders. Another search-party arrives, this time led by Brabantio, who accuses and insults Othello. The Moor maintains his dignity, and it is decided to discuss matters before the Duke.

1 *trade of war*: as a professional soldier.
2 *very stuff*: the essence.
3 *contrived*: calculated, in cold blood.
   iniquity: evil-mindedness.
4 *to do me service*: for my own good.
5 *yerked*: thrust at.
   him: Iago speaks of Roderigo.
6 *'Tis better as it is*: Othello speaks calmly, in contrast to Iago's lying excitement.
6 *prated*: talked nonsense.
7 *scurvy*: insulting.
10 *full hard*: with difficulty.
11 *fast*: definitely.
12 *Magnifico*: Venetian nobleman (i.e. Brabantio).
13 *hath … potential*: has a voice whose effect is very powerful.
14 *double*: influential (perhaps the Duke had twice as much power as an ordinary senator—and likewise Brabantio).
15 *grievance*: hardship.
17 *give him cable*: allow him.
   do his spite: the worst that his spite can do; Othello is still calm and speaks with great dignity.
18 *the signory*: the Venetian government.
19 *out-tongue*: speak louder than.
   'Tis yet to know: No one knows yet.
20 *when … honour*: when I learn that boasting is an honourable thing to do; Othello is restrained and modest about his birth and achievements.
21 *provulgate*: make generally known.
22 *siege*: rank.
   demerits: deserts.
23 *speak*: lay claim.
   unbonneted: on equal terms (without my hat on).
26 *unhousèd*: unfettered (without the ties of property).

Scene 2

Enter Othello, Iago, Attendants *with torches*

Iago
Though in the trade of war I have slain men,
Yet do I hold it very stuff o'th'conscience
To do no contrived murder: I lack iniquity
Sometimes to do me service. Nine or ten times
5 I had thought t'have yerked him here under the ribs.
Othello
'Tis better as it is.
Iago   Nay, but he prated
And spoke such scurvy and provoking terms
Against your honour,
That with the little godliness I have,
10 I did full hard forbear him. But I pray, sir,
Are you fast married? For be assured of this,
That the Magnifico is much beloved,
And hath in his effect a voice potential
As double as the Duke's. He will divorce you,
15 Or put upon you what restraint and grievance
That law, with all his might to enforce it on,
Will give him cable.
Othello   Let him do his spite:
My services, which I have done the signory,
Shall out-tongue his complaints. 'Tis yet to know—
20 Which, when I know that boasting is an honour,
I shall provulgate—I fetch my life and being
From men of royal siege, and my demerits
May speak, unbonneted, to as proud a fortune
As this that I have reached. For know, Iago,
25 But that I love the gentle Desdemona,
I would not my unhousèd free condition
Put into circumscription and confine
For the seas' worth. But look, what lights come
    yond!
Iago
Those are the raisèd father and his friends:
30 You were best go in.
Othello   Not I: I must be found.
My parts, my title, and my perfect soul
Shall manifest me rightly. Is it they?

27 *into ... confine*: under restriction and restraint.
28 *yond*: yonder.
29 *raisèd*: alarmed.
30 Iago counsels flight, but Othello is fearless.
31 *parts*: natural qualities.
   title: entitlement, rights (as Desdemona's husband)
   perfect soul: clear conscience.
33 *Janus*: Iago swears, appropriately, by the two-faced Roman god.
37 *haste-post-haste*: speediest possible.

39 *divine*: guess.
40 *heat*: urgency.
41 *sequent*: one after the other.

44 *hotly*: urgently.

46 *several*: separate.

49 *makes he here*: is he doing here; Cassio appears not to know of Othello's marriage, although we are told later (in *Act 2*) that he accompanied Othello when he was courting Desdemona.
50 *'Faith*: In faith, indeed.
   boarded: taken possession of.
   carack: treasure ship.
51 *made*: financially secure.

53 *Marry*: Iago swears by the Virgin Mary (and perhaps puns on 'marry' = wed).
   Have with you: 'I'll go with you'.

54 *for you*: ready to fight with you.

Iago
By Janus, I think no.

Enter Cassio, *with* Men *bearing torches*

Othello
The servants of the Duke and my lieutenant!
35 The goodness of the night upon you, friends.
What is the news?
      Cassio   The Duke does greet you, general,
And he requires your haste-post-haste appearance
Even on the instant.
      Othello   What is the matter, think you?
      Cassio
Something from Cyprus, as I may divine:
40 It is a business of some heat. The galleys
Have sent a dozen sequent messengers
This very night at one another's heels;
And many of the consuls, raised and met,
Are at the Duke's already. You have been hotly
      called for,
45 When being not at your lodging to be found.
The senate hath sent about three several quests
To search you out.
      Othello   'Tis well I am found by you:
I will but spend a word here in the house
And go with you.   [*Exit*
      Cassio   Ancient, what makes he here?
      Iago
50 Faith, he tonight hath boarded a land carack:
If it prove lawful prize, he's made for ever.
      Cassio
I do not understand.
      Iago   He's married.
      Cassio   To who?
      Iago
Marry, to—Come, captain, will you go?

Enter Othello

Othello   Have with you.
Cassio
Here comes another troop to seek for you.

Enter Brabantio, Roderigo, *with* Officers *and torches*

59 *Keep up*: Put away; Othello silences the hostile Venetians with a few words of authority.
60 *with years*: because of your age.
62 *stowed*: hidden.
63 *enchanted*: bewitched.
64 *refer me*: appeal.
    all things of sense: any common sense.
67 *opposite*: opposed.
68 *curlèd*: with curled hair—attractive.
    darlings: favourites.
69 *a general mock*: everybody's scorn.
70 *guardage*: guardianship.
72 *Judge me the world*: Let all the world judge for me.
    gross in sense: quite obvious.
73 *practised*: performed.
74 *minerals*: i.e. poisonous substances.
75 *motion*: will-power.
    disputed on: formally (legally) discussed.
76 *probable*: can be proved.
    palpable to thinking: may very easily be thought.
77 *apprehend*: seize.
    attach: arrest.
78 *abuser*: corrupter.
    the world: i.e. Venetian society.
79 *arts inhibited*: forbidden arts—i.e. black magic.
    out of warrant: unlawful.
81 *at his peril*: at whatever risk to Othello.
82 *of my inclining*: on my side.
83-4 *cue ... prompter*: Othello uses the language of the theatre—without being in the least 'theatrical'.
84 *will you*: do you wish?

Iago
55 It is Brabantio: general, be advised,
    He comes to bad intent.
        Othello   Holla, stand there.
        Roderigo
    Signor, it is the Moor.
        Brabantio   Down with him, thief!
        Iago
    You, Roderigo? Come, sir, I am for you.
        Othello
    Keep up your bright swords, for the dew will rust
        them.
60 Good signor, you shall more command with years
    Than with your weapons.
        Brabantio
    O thou foul thief! Where hast thou stowed my
        daughter?
    Damned as thou art, thou hast enchanted her:
    For I'll refer me to all things of sense,
65 If she in chains of magic were not bound,
    Whether a maid, so tender, fair, and happy,
    So opposite to marriage that she shunned
    The wealthy curlèd darlings of our nation,
    Would ever have—t'incur a general mock—
70 Run from her guardage to the sooty bosom
    Of such a thing as thou: to fear, not to delight.
    Judge me the world, if 'tis not gross in sense
    That thou hast practised on her with foul charms,
    Abused her delicate youth with drugs or minerals
75 That weakens motion. I'll have't disputed on;
    'Tis probable, and palpable to thinking:
    I therefore apprehend, and do attach thee
    For an abuser of the world, a practiser
    Of arts inhibited, and out of warrant.
80 Lay hold upon him: if he do resist,
    Subdue him, at his peril.
        Othello   Hold your hands,
    Both you of my inclining and the rest.
    Were it my cue to fight, I should have known it
    Without a prompter. Where will you that I go
85 To answer this your charge?

86 *course*: procedure.
  direct session: immediate trial.
90 *present*: urgent.
94 *In*: At.
  Bring: Take.
95 *idle*: trivial.
96 *brothers of the state*: i.e. the nobility of
  Venice.
98 *passage free*: free pardon.
99 *Bondslaves*: We learn in the next scene that
  Othello had been a slave.

Brabantio   To prison, till fit time
Of law and course of direct session
Call thee to answer.
    Othello   What if I do obey?
How may the Duke be therewith satisfied?
Whose messengers are here about my side,
90 Upon some present business of the state
To bring me to him?
    Officer   'Tis true, most worthy signor:
The Duke's in council, and your noble self
I am sure is sent for.
    Brabantio   How? The Duke in council?
In this time of the night? Bring him away.
95 Mine's not an idle cause; the Duke himself,
Or any of my brothers of the state,
Cannot but feel this wrong as 'twere their own:
For if such actions may have passage free,
Bondslaves and pagans shall our statesmen be.
                              [*Exeunt*

Act 1   Scene 3

The Duke and the Venetian senators are
trying to assess the power of the Turkish
fleet: reports are contradictory, and it is not
even sure whether the ships are heading for
Cyprus or for Rhodes. A message from the
Governor of Cyprus settles the problems.
But the meeting is interrupted by the angry
Brabantio, who accuses Othello of having
seduced Desdemona and stolen her away
from her father. The Moor defends himself
with powerful dignity. The Duke is
impressed, especially when Othello speaks of
his courtship; after Desdemona has declared
her love for Othello the Duke gives his
blessing to the marriage, and speaks words
of consolation to Brabantio. He commissions
Othello with the leadership of the Venetian
force against the Turks, and Desdemona
requests permission to accompany her
husband to Cyprus. When the senators and
the lovers have departed, Iago gives his own
interpretation of the episode, urging
Roderigo to make further efforts to win
Desdemona. Finally Iago is alone on the
stage, and he voices his plans for ruining the
happiness of Othello and Desdemona.

Scene 3

The Duke *and* Senators *sitting at a table;
with lights and* Attendants

    Duke
There is no composition in these news
That gives them credit.
    First Senator   Indeed they are disproportioned.
My letters say a hundred and seven galleys.
    Duke
And mine, a hundred and forty.
    Second Senator   And mine two hundred;
5 But though they jump not on a just accompt—
As in these cases where the aim reports

1 *composition*: agreement; the inconsistency of
   the different reports is itself very worrying.
   news: reports.
2 *gives them credit*: makes them credible.
   disproportioned: inconsistent.
5 *jump not*: do not agree.
   just accompt: precise reckoning.
6 *the aim reports*: the reckoning is given by
   guesswork.
8 *bearing up*: sailing towards.
9 *possible enough to judgement*: understandable.
10 *secure me in the error*: allow myself to feel
   safe because of the mistake (i.e. in giving
   the number of ships).
11 *article*: issue.
   approve: accept.
12 *in fearful sense*: with a feeling of fear.
14 *preparation*: force.
   makes for: is heading towards.
16 *Signor Angelo*: Presumably this is some
   naval commander; he is not mentioned
   again.
17 *How say you*: What do you think of.
   change: i.e. of direction—the fleet was first
   said to be sailing towards Cyprus.
18 *assay*: test; the Senator's language is formal
   and pompous.
   pageant: show.
19 *in false gaze*: looking the wrong way.
20 *importancy*: importance.
21-6 Not only is Cyprus more important than
   Rhodes, but it is also easier for the Turks
   to capture it.
23 *facile question*: easy attack.
   bear: capture.
24 *For that*: since.
   brace: readiness.
25 *abilities*: equipment.
26 *dressed in*: ready with.
   make thought: consider.
28 *latest*: last.
29 *an ... gain*: to try something that will be
   easy and profitable.
30 *wage*: risk, gamble with.
31 No, we can be sure he's not heading for
   Rhodes.
33 *Ottomites*: Turks (from the Ottoman
   Empire).
   reverend and gracious: The Messenger
   addresses the Duke.

'Tis oft with difference—yet do they all confirm
A Turkish fleet, and bearing up to Cyprus.
    Duke
Nay, it is possible enough to judgement:
10 I do not so secure me in the error,
But the main article I do approve
In fearful sense.
    Sailor [*Without*]   What ho! What ho! What ho!
    First Officer
A messenger from the galleys.

    Enter Sailor

    Duke   Now, what's the business?
    Sailor
The Turkish preparation makes for Rhodes;
15 So was I bid report here to the state
By Signor Angelo.
    Duke
How say you by this change?
    First Senator   This cannot be,
By no assay of reason. 'Tis a pageant
To keep us in false gaze. When we consider
20 Th'importancy of Cyprus to the Turk,
And let ourselves again but understand
That as it more concerns the Turk than Rhodes,
So may he with more facile question bear it,
For that it stands not in such warlike brace,
25 But altogether lacks th'abilities
That Rhodes is dressed in. If we make thought of
   this,
We must not think the Turk is so unskilful
To leave that latest which concerns him first,
Neglecting an attempt of ease and gain
30 To wake and wage a danger profitless.
    Duke
Nay, in all confidence he's not for Rhodes.
    First Officer
Here is more news.

    Enter a Messenger

    Messenger
The Ottomites, reverend and gracious,
Steering with due course towards the isle of Rhodes,

35 *injointed*: linked up.
    after: following.

37 *sail*: ships.
    re-stem: retrace.
38 *with frank appearance*: undisguised.
39 *Signor Montano*: The Governor of Cyprus.
40 *servitor*: servant.
41 *with ... thus*: This is not just another spy's
    report, but an official message—with words
    of formal greeting—from Montano.

44 *Marcus Luccicos*: Another unknown
    —probably military—character who
    is never heard of again.

49 *general*: public.

52 *Good your grace*: A formal address to the
    Duke.
53 *place*: i.e. as a senator.

55 *Take hold on me*: worry me.
    particular: personal.
56 *flood-gate*: When the flood-gates are
    opened, the torrent pours through them.
    o'erbearing: overwhelming.
57 *engluts*: engulfs.
59 *My daughter*: Brabantio's distress breaks
    through the restraints of his formal speech.

35 Have there injointed with an after fleet.
    First Senator
    Ay, so I thought. How many, as you guess?
    Messenger
    Of thirty sail; and now they do re-stem
    Their backward course, bearing with frank
        appearance
    Their purposes towards Cyprus. Signor Montano,
40 Your trusty and most valiant servitor,
    With his free duty recommends you thus,
    And prays you to believe him.
    Duke
    'Tis certain then for Cyprus.
    Marcus Luccicos, is not he in town?
    First Senator
45 He's now in Florence.
    Duke   Write from us: wish him
    Post-post-haste dispatch.
    First Senator
    Here comes Brabantio and the valiant Moor.

    Enter Brabantio, Othello, Iago, Roderigo,
    and Officers

    Duke
    Valiant Othello, we must straight employ you
    Against the general enemy Ottoman.
50 [*To* Brabantio] I did not see you: welcome, gentle
        signor;
    We lacked your counsel and your help tonight.
    Brabantio
    So did I yours. Good your grace, pardon me:
    Neither my place, nor aught I heard of business,
    Hath raised me from my bed; nor doth the general
        care
55 Take hold on me; for my particular grief
    Is of so flood-gate and o'erbearing nature
    That it engluts and swallows other sorrows
    And yet is still itself.
    Duke   Why? What's the matter?
    Brabantio
    My daughter! O, my daughter!
    Senators   Dead?

Brabantio   Ay, to me.
60 She is abused, stolen from me, and corrupted
By spells and medicines bought of mountebanks;
For nature so preposterously to err,
Being not deficient, blind, or lame of sense,
Sans witchcraft could not.
Duke
65 Whoe'er he be that in this foul proceeding
Hath thus beguiled your daughter of herself
And you of her, the bloody book of law
You shall yourself read in the bitter letter
After your own sense, yea, though our proper son
70 Stood in your action.
Brabantio   Humbly I thank your grace.
Here is the man: this Moor, whom now it seems
Your special mandate for the state affairs
Hath hither brought.
All   We are very sorry for't.
Duke
What in your own part can you say to this?
Brabantio
75 Nothing, but this is so.
Othello
Most potent, grave and reverend signors,
My very noble and approved good masters,
That I have ta'en away this old man's daughter,
It is most true; true I have married her;
80 The very head and front of my offending
Hath this extent, no more. Rude am I in my speech
And little blessed with the soft phrase of peace;
For since these arms of mine had seven years' pith
Till now some nine moons wasted, they have used
85 Their dearest action in the tented field;
And little of the great world can I speak
More than pertains to feats of broil and battle;
And therefore little shall I grace my cause
In speaking for myself. Yet, by your gracious
        patience,

61 *of mountebanks*: from quack doctors.
62 *preposterously*: unnaturally; Brabantio
    emphasizes the strangeness of Desdemona's
    behaviour, suggesting that she must be
    under the influence of drugs or witchcraft.
    to err: to stray from itself.
63 *deficient*: morally defective.
    lame of sense: lacking in intelligence.
64 *Sans*: Without.
66 *beguiled ... herself*: cheated your daughter
    out of her senses.
67–9 The Duke seems to be promising that
    Brabantio shall himself act as judge and
    pronounce the grim sentence written in the
    legal statutes.
69 *proper*: own.
70 *Stood ... action*: Was named in your
    accusation.
72 *mandate*: order.
74 *part*: defence.
75 Brabantio's impatient interruption
    increases the tension before Othello can
    speak.
76 *potent*: mighty.
    reverend: respected.
77 *approved*: esteemed.
    masters: Othello pays great respect to the
    senators, acknowledging their power over
    him—he is their servant.
80 *head and front*: height and breadth (i.e. the
    full extent); Othello uses military terms.
81 *Rude*: Plain; Othello's language must be
    compared with the complicated phrasing of
    the First Senator's speeches, or even those
    of Roderigo.
82 *soft phrase of peace*: elegant diction of
    civilians.
83 *pith*: strength.
84 *moons*: months.
    wasted: past.
    used: been accustomed to doing.
85 *dearest action*: most important work.
    tented field: battlefield (where the armies
    pitched their tents).
87 *broil*: fighting.

90 *round*: plain.
   unvarnished: without decoration.

92 *conjuration*: incantations.
93 *charged withal*: accused of.

95 *motion*: desire.

97 *credit*: reputation.

99–101 *It is ... nature*: Only a warped
   imagination could believe that one so
   perfect [as Desdemona] could fall into such
   unnatural error.
101 *must be driven*: The subject of the verb is
   'one' (= any reasonable person).
102 *find out*: suggest.
103 *vouch*: assert.
105 *dram ... effect*: magic potion concocted for
   this purpose.
106 *wrought*: worked a spell.
   vouch: assert.
107 *more wider*: fuller.
   overt test: obvious evidence.
108 *these ... likelihoods*: rather poorly presented
   (thinly clad) guesswork.
109 *Of modern seeming*: About what appears
   quite ordinary.
   prefer: object.
111 *by indirect ... courses*: by cunning and
   force.
112 *Subdue*: Seduce.
113 *request*: consent.
   fair question: honest discussion.

117 *foul*: wicked, culpable.

122–3 *as truly ... blood*: Othello confesses his
   sins to God—a regular part of Christian
   worship.

90   I will a round unvarnished tale deliver
     Of my whole course of love: what drugs, what
        charms,
     What conjuration and what mighty magic—
     For such proceedings I am charged withal—
     I won his daughter.
     Brabantio   A maiden never bold;
95   Of spirit so still and quiet that her motion
     Blushed at herself: and she, in spite of nature,
     Of years, of country, credit, everything,
     To fall in love with what she feared to look on!
     It is a judgement maimed and most imperfect
100 That will confess perfection so could err
     Against all rules of nature, and must be driven
     To find out practices of cunning hell
     Why this should be. I therefore vouch again
     That with some mixtures powerful o'er the blood,
105 Or with some dram conjured to this effect,
     He wrought upon her.
     Duke   To vouch this is no proof,
     Without more wider and more overt test
     Than these thin habits and poor likelihoods
     Of modern seeming do prefer against him.
     First Senator
110 But, Othello, speak:
     Did you by indirect and forcèd courses
     Subdue and poison this young maid's affections?
     Or came it by request and such fair question
     As soul to soul affordeth?
     Othello   I do beseech you,
115 Send for the lady to the Sagittary,
     And let her speak of me before her father.
     If you do find me foul in her report,
     The trust, the office I do hold of you
     Not only take away, but let your sentence
120 Even fall upon my life.
     Duke   Fetch Desdemona hither.
     Othello
     Ancient, conduct them: you best know the place.
                    [*Exit* Iago *with* Attendants
     And till she come, as truly as to heaven
     I do confess the vices of my blood,
     So justly to your grave ears I'll present

125 *thrive*: proceed.
131 *ran it through*: recounted it all.
     even ... boyish days: right from my childhood.
133 *chances*: happenings.
134 *moving accidents*: exciting adventures.
     by flood and field: on sea and land.
135 *hair-breadth scapes*: narrow escapes.
     i'th'imminent deadly breach: in that dangerous moment when a fortification is broken open.
137 *redemption*: rescue (by being ransomed).
138 *portance*: conduct.
139 *antres*: caves.
     idle: barren.
141 *process*: narrative.
143 *Anthropophagi*: Man-eaters.

145 *incline*: bow her head, listening intently ('seriously').
146 *still*: always.
     house affairs: household chores.
147 As soon as she could get them done.
148 *again*: back.
150 *pliant hour*: favourable moment.
151 *prayer of earnest heart*: sincere request.
152 *pilgrimage*: travels.
     dilate: recount in detail.
153 *by parcels*: in bits.
154 *intentively*: altogether, paying proper attention.
155 *beguile her of her tears*: steal tears from her, cause her to weep.
158 *pains*: troubles.
159 *passing*: very.
160 *wondrous*: exceedingly.
162 *made her such a man*: This could mean *either* 'made her a man so that she could be like Othello'; *or* 'made such a man for her husband'.

125 How I did thrive in this fair lady's love,
     And she in mine.
       Duke   Say it, Othello.
       Othello
     Her father loved me, oft invited me,
     Still questioned me the story of my life
     From year to year—the battles, sieges, fortunes
130 That I have passed.
     I ran it through, even from my boyish days
     To th'very moment that he bade me tell it:
     Wherein I spake of most disastrous chances,
     Of moving accidents by flood and field,
135 Of hair-breadth scapes i'th'imminent deadly breach,
     Of being taken by the insolent foe,
     And sold to slavery; of my redemption thence,
     And portance in my travels' history:
     Wherein of antres vast and deserts idle,
140 Rough quarries, rocks, and hills whose heads touch heaven,
     It was my hint to speak—such was the process:
     And of the Cannibals that each other eat,
     The Anthropophagi, and men whose heads
     Do grow beneath their shoulders. This to hear
145 Would Desdemona seriously incline:
     But still the house affairs would draw her thence,
     Which ever as she could with haste dispatch
     She'd come again, and with a greedy ear
     Devour up my discourse; which I observing
150 Took once a pliant hour, and found good means
     To draw from her a prayer of earnest heart
     That I would all my pilgrimage dilate
     Whereof by parcels she had something heard,
     But not intentively. I did consent,
155 And often did beguile her of her tears
     When I did speak of some distressful stroke
     That my youth suffered. My story being done,
     She gave me for my pains a world of sighs:
     She swore, in faith 'twas strange, 'twas passing strange,
160 'Twas pitiful, 'twas wondrous pitiful;
     She wished she had not heard it, yet she wished
     That heaven had made her such a man. She thanked me,

165 *hint*: opportunity.
166 *passed*: endured.
167 *that*: because.

169 *witness*: give evidence.

171 *take ... best*: make the best of a bad job.

172-3 It is better to use a weapon which is broken than no weapon at all (i.e. 'bare hands').
174 *half the wooer*: i.e. shared the responsibility for her seduction.
175 *bad blame*: curse.
176 *Light*: Fall
179 *a divided duty*: In another play, *King Lear*, Shakespeare shows a great interest in the triangular relationship of father—daughter—husband.
180 *education*: upbringing.
181 *learn*: instruct me.
183 *hitherto*: so far.
186 *challenge*: claim.
187 *God bu'y*: God be with you.
188 May it please your grace, let's get on with affairs of state.
189 *get*: beget.
191 *that*: something (i.e. Desdemona).
192 *but thou hast already*: except that you have it already.
194 *at soul*: in my heart.
195 *escape*: elopement.
196 *clogs*: blocks of wood fastened to the legs of horses to prevent their escape.
197 *like yourself*: like your better self—the Duke appeals to Brabantio's reason and commonsense.
   lay a sentence: speak some words of wisdom; the Duke proceeds to utter a series of banal commonplaces. The rhymes of the couplets, and their heavy rhythm, emphasize the trite words—and it is not surprising that Brabantio finds no comfort in them.

And bade me, if I had a friend that loved her,
I should but teach him how to tell my story,
165 And that would woo her. Upon this hint I spake:
She loved me for the dangers I had passed,
And I loved her, that she did pity them.
This only is the witchcraft I have used.
Here comes the lady: let her witness it.

Enter Desdemona, Iago, *and* Attendants

Duke
170 I think this tale would win my daughter too.
Good Brabantio, take up this mangled matter at the best:
Men do their broken weapons rather use
Than their bare hands.
Brabantio   I pray you hear her speak.
If she confess that she was half the wooer,
175 Destruction on my head, if my bad blame
Light on the man! Come hither, gentle mistress;
Do you perceive in all this company
Where most you owe obedience?
Desdemona   My noble father,
I do perceive here a divided duty:
180 To you I am bound for life and education;
My life and education both do learn me
How to respect you. You are lord of all my duty,
I am hitherto your daughter. But here's my husband;
And so much duty as my mother showed
185 To you, preferring you before her father,
So much I challenge, that I may profess
Due to the Moor, my lord.
Brabantio   God bu'y! I have done.
Please it your grace, on to the state affairs.
I had rather to adopt a child than get it.
190 Come hither, Moor:
I here do give thee that with all my heart
Which, but thou hast already, with all my heart
I would keep from thee. For your sake, jewel,
I am glad at soul I have no other child,
195 For thy escape would teach me tyranny
To hang clogs on them. I have done, my lord.
Duke
Let me speak like yourself and lay a sentence

198   *grise*: another word for 'step'.
200-1   The troubles ('griefs') are over when we know the cure ('remedies') we hoped for until recently ('late') is impossible, and the worst has happened.
202   *mischief*: problem.
203   *next way*: best way.
        draw ... on: cause more problems.
204-5   If you can't keep something that pure chance takes from you, you can scoff at the loss ('injury') by accepting it with patience.
206   A man who has been robbed and yet smiles, deprives the thief of something.
207   *bootless*: useless.
208   *So*: In that case; Brabantio parodies the Duke's words of wisdom.
        beguile: cheat.
210-11   A man can suffer (bear) this moralizing ('sentence') well when he has nothing except this easy advice to suffer.
213   *pay grief*: in order to endure his sorrow.
        poor patience borrow: has to resort to mere patience.
214   *to sugar ... gall*: whether sweet or bitter.
215   *equivocal*: of equal value.
217   *piecèd*: mended.
        through the ear: by talking.
218   *proceed to*: get on with.
219-26   After the rhymes, it is refreshing to find a speech in prose where the Duke adopts a more businesslike manner.
219   *preparation*: armed force.
        makes for: is heading towards.
220   *fortitude*: strength.

Which as a grise or step may help these lovers
Into your favour.
200   When remedies are past the griefs are ended
By seeing the worst which late on hopes depended.
To mourn a mischief that is past and gone
Is the next way to draw new mischief on.
What cannot be preserved when fortune takes,
205   Patience her injury a mockery makes.
The robbed that smiles steals something from the
        thief;
He robs himself that spends a bootless grief.

Brabantio
So let the Turk of Cyprus us beguile,
We lose it not so long as we can smile;
210   He bears the sentence well that nothing bears
But the free comfort which from thence he hears;
But he bears both the sentence and the sorrow
That to pay grief must of poor patience borrow.
These sentences, to sugar or to gall
215   Being strong on both sides, are equivocal.
But words are words; I never yet did hear
That the bruised heart was piecèd through the ear.
I humbly beseech you proceed to th'affairs of state.

Duke
The Turk with a most mighty preparation makes for
220   Cyprus. Othello, the fortitude of the place is best
known to you: and though we have there a substitute of

221 *substitute*: deputy, i.e. Montano.
222 *allowed sufficiency*: recognized efficiency.
    opinion: public opinion.
222–3 *a more ... effects*: which makes the final
    decision in these matters.
223 *throws ... you*: votes for you as the safer
    choice.
224 *slubber*: tarnish.
225 *more stubborn*: tougher.
    boisterous: violent.
226 *expedition*: assignment.
228 *flinty and steel*: rough and hard.
229 *thrice-driven ... down*: like a bed of the
    finest down (made by three times fanning
    the feathers to get the very lightest down).
    I do agnize: recognize in myself.
230–1 *A natural ... hardness*: A natural
    inclination and readiness for hardship.
233 *bending ... state*: bowing to your authority.
234 *disposition*: arrangements.
235 *Due ... place*: treatment appropriate to her
    position.
    exhibition: financial allowance.
236 *besort*: service.
237 *levels*: suits.
241 *in his eye*: in his sight.
242 *unfolding*: proposal.
    lend ... ear: listen favourably.
243 *charter*: permission.
244 *simpleness*: innocence.
246 *downright violence*: bold action.
    scorn of fortunes: disregard of money and
    social position; the Folio text reads
    'storm'—see p.iv
247 *trumpet*: boldly declare.
    subdued: obedient.
248 *Even ... lord*: To whatever it is that
    Othello wants; the Folio text reads 'very
    quality'—see p.iv
249 *Othello's ... mind*: Othello's mind, not his
    face, is what mattered to Desdemona.
250 *parts*: qualities.
253 *A moth*: Moths, although pretty, are
    useless; they may even be destructive.
254 *rites*: i.e. the marriage rites—her sexual
    pleasure with her husband.
    bereft me: taken away from me.
255 *heavy interim*: boring interval.
    support: endure.

256 *his dear absence*: the absence of one who is
    dear.

most allowed sufficiency, yet opinion, a more sovereign
mistress of effects, throws a more safer voice on you.
You must therefore be content to slubber the gloss of
225 your new fortunes with this more stubborn and
boisterous expedition.

    Othello
The tyrant custom, most grave senators,
Hath made the flinty and steel couch of war
My thrice-driven bed of down. I do agnize
230 A natural and prompt alacrity
I find in hardness; and do undertake
This present war against the Ottomites.
Most humbly, therefore, bending to your state,
I crave fit disposition for my wife,
235 Due reference of place and exhibition,
With such accommodation and besort
As levels with her breeding.
    Duke   If you please,
Be't at her father's.
    Brabantio   I'll not have it so.
    Othello
Nor I.
    Desdemona   Nor I: I would not there reside
240 To put my father in impatient thoughts
By being in his eye. Most gracious Duke,
To my unfolding lend your prosperous ear,
And let me find a charter in your voice
T'assist my simpleness.
    Duke   What would you? Speak.
    Desdemona
245 That I did love the Moor to live with him,
My downright violence and scorn of fortunes
May trumpet to the world. My heart's subdued
Even to the utmost pleasure of my lord.
I saw Othello's visage in his mind
250 And to his honours and his valiant parts
Did I my soul and fortunes consecrate.
So that, dear lords, if I be left behind
A moth of peace, and he go to the war,
The rites for which I love him are bereft me,
255 And I a heavy interim shall support
By his dear absence. Let me go with him.

257 *voice*: approval.
258 *Vouch with me, heaven*: As heaven is my witness.
259–62 These lines have puzzled many commentators; I think Othello is requesting Desdemona's company not because she is the particular object of his passion and would 'please the palate of my desire', and not because he needs a woman to satisfy ('comply with') the natural desires ('heat') of his body—which are not so urgent now that the passions ('affects') of youth are dead ('defunct'); nor even to give him the 'proper satisfaction' that the wife should give to her husband. Rather he wants to enjoy her company—her 'mind'.
263 *that you think*: if you think.
264 *scant*: neglect.
265 *For*: Because.
    light-winged toys: trivialities.
266 *feathered Cupid*: The Roman god of love is depicted as a blindfolded, winged boy.
    seel: close up.
    wanton dullness: frivolous blindness.
267 *speculative and officed instruments*: his mind and eyes, which are intended to think ('speculative'), and have been given a job to do ('officed').
268 *disports*: enjoyments.
    taint: spoil.
269 *skillet*: saucepan.
    helm: helmet.
270 *indign*: unworthy.
271 *Make head against*: Attack.
    estimation: reputation.
272 *privately determine*: personally decide.
273 *cries*: demands.
278 *commission*: the official documents.
279 *of quality and respect*: which are important and relevant.
280 *import*: concern.
    my ancient: Othello introduces Iago to the Duke.
282 *conveyance*: escort.
283 *needful*: necessary.
286 *If ... lack*: If virtue in itself is beautiful.
    delighted: charming.

Othello
Let her have your voice.
Vouch with me, heaven, I therefore beg it not
To please the palate of my appetite,
260 Nor to comply with heat—the young affects
In me defunct—and proper satisfaction;
But to be free and bounteous to her mind.
And heaven defend your good souls that you think
I will your serious and great business scant
265 For she is with me. No, when light-winged toys
Of feathered Cupid seel with wanton dullness
My speculative and officed instruments,
That my disports corrupt and taint my business,
Let housewives make a skillet of my helm,
270 And all indign and base adversities.
Make head against my estimation!
    Duke
Be it as you shall privately determine,
Either for her stay, or going. Th'affair cries haste,
And speed must answer it. You must hence tonight.
    Desdemona
275 Tonight, my lord?
    Duke   This night.
    Othello   With all my heart.
    Duke
At nine i'th'morning, here we'll meet again.
Othello, leave some officer behind,
And he shall our commission bring to you,
With such things else of quality and respect
280 As doth import you.
    Othello   So please your grace, my ancient;
A man he is of honesty and trust:
To his conveyance I assign my wife,
With what else needful your good grace shall think
To be sent after me.
    Duke   Let it be so.
285 Good night to everyone. And, noble signor,
If virtue no delighted beauty lack,
Your son-in-law is far more fair than black.
    First Senator
Adieu, brave Moor: use Desdemona well.

Brabantio
Look to her, Moor, if thou hast eyes to see.
290   She has deceived her father, and may thee.
Othello
My life upon her faith!
             [*Exeunt* Duke, Senators, *and* Attendants
                             Honest Iago,
My Desdemona must I leave to thee.
I prithee let thy wife attend on her,
And bring them after in the best advantage.
295   Come, Desdemona, I have but an hour
Of love, of worldly matters, and direction
To spend with thee. We must obey the time.
             [*Exeunt* Othello *and* Desdemona
Roderigo
Iago.
Iago
What says't thou, noble heart?
Roderigo
300   What will I do, think'st thou?
Iago
Why, go to bed and sleep.
Roderigo
I will incontinently drown myself.
Iago
If thou dost, I shall never love thee after. Why, thou
silly gentleman?
Roderigo
305   It is silliness to live, when to live is torment: and then
we have a prescription to die, when death is our
physician.
Iago
O villainous! I have looked upon the world for four
times seven years, and since I could distinguish betwixt
310   a benefit and an injury, I never found a man that knew
how to love himself. Ere I would say I would drown
myself for the love of a guinea-hen, I would change my
humanity with a baboon.
Roderigo
What should I do? I confess it is my shame to be so
315   fond, but it is not in my virtue to amend it.
Iago
Virtue? A fig! 'Tis in ourselves that we are thus, or

---

291 *My life ... faith*: Othello would stake his life on Desdemona's faithfulness.

292 *to thee*: to your care.
293 *prithee*: pray you.
294 *in the best advantage*: at the most convenient time.
295 *but*: only.
296 *worldly matters*: business.
       direction: instructions.
297 *obey the time*: do what the situation demands.

298–376 The formal dignity of the ducal court gives place to the colloquial cynicism of Iago's conversation with Roderigo.

300 *will*: shall.

302 *incontinently*: immediately.

303 *after*: afterwards.
304 *silly*: simple-minded.

306 *prescription*: doctor's order.

311 *Ere*: Before.
312 *guinea-hen*: woman; the term is abusive, and suggests that the woman can be bought; but it is not as strong as 'prostitute'.
314–5 *my shame ... so fond*: I am ashamed to be so foolish.
315 *virtue*: power.
316 *Virtue*: Iago uses the word with overtones of morality.
       a fig: a contemptuous remark, usually accompanied with an obscene gesture.

319 *set*: plant.
320 *gender*: kind.
       distract: vary.
321 *sterile with idleness*: barren because we are too lazy to look after them.
322 *corrigible*: correcting.
323 *beam*: balance; the image is of weighing-scales, in which two pans are suspended from a beam and balanced against each other.
324 *scale*: weighing-pan.
       poise: counterpoise.
326 *preposterous*: unnatural.
327 *motions*: desires.
       carnal stings: fleshly urges.
328 *unbitted*: unbridled.
329 *sect or scion*: cutting or graft.
331-2 *permission of the will*: i.e. Roderigo could control the lust of his blood, but his will gives consent to his desire.
333 *blind puppies*: unwanted puppies are drowned as soon as they are born, before their eyes have opened.
334 *deserving*: deserts.
335 *perdurable*: everlasting.
       stead: help.
336 *Follow ... wars*: Follow Othello to the war in Cyprus.
337 *Defeat ... beard*: Hide your face with a false beard (the implication is that Roderigo is not man enough to grow his own beard).
339 *long continue her love*: go on loving for a long time.
341 *answerable sequestration*: corresponding separation.
342 *put but money*: just put money.
345 *locusts*: carobs (a sweet Mediterranean fruit).
       acerbe: bitter.
346 *the coloquintida*: the bitter-apple (colocynth), used as a purgative.
       for youth: for a younger man.
349 *damn thyself*: i.e. by committing suicide, which is forbidden by God.
350 *sanctimony*: piety.
351 *a frail vow*: Iago is contemptuous of the marriage vows.
       erring: pagan.
       super-subtle: over-sophisticated.
352-3 *the tribe of hell*: the devils; Iago seems to place himself amongst the devils.
353 *enjoy her*: i.e. sexually.
354 *A pox of drowning thyself*: Iago is contemptuous.

thus. Our bodies are our gardens, to the which our wills are gardeners. So that if we plant nettles or sow lettuce, set hyssop and weed up thyme, supply it 320 with one gender of herbs or distract it with many, either to have it sterile with idleness or manured with industry, why the power and corrigible authority of this lies in our wills. If the beam of our lives had not one scale of reason to poise another of sensuality, 325 the blood and baseness of our natures would conduct us to most preposterous conclusions. But we have reason to cool our raging motions, our carnal stings, our unbitted lusts: whereof I take this, that you call love, to be a sect or scion.

Roderigo
330 It cannot be.

Iago
It is merely a lust of the blood and a permission of the will. Come, be a man. Drown thyself? Drown cats and blind puppies. I have professed me thy friend, and I confess me knit to thy deserving with cables of 335 perdurable toughness. I could never better stead thee than now. Put money in thy purse. Follow thou these wars; defeat thy favour with an usurped beard. I say, put money in thy purse. It cannot be that Desdemona should long continue her love to the Moor—put 340 money in thy purse—nor he his to her. It was a violent commencement, and thou shalt see an answerable sequestration—put but money in thy purse. These Moors are changeable in their wills—fill thy purse with money. The food that to him now is as luscious 345 as locusts shall be to him shortly as acerbe as the coloquintida. She must change for youth: when she is sated with his body she will find the error of her choice. Therefore put money in thy purse. If thou wilt needs damn thyself, do it a more delicate way than drowning. 350 Make all the money thou canst. If sanctimony and a frail vow betwixt an erring barbarian and a super-subtle Venetian be not too hard for my wits and all the tribe of hell, thou shalt enjoy her—therefore make money. A pox of drowning thyself! It is clean out of the way. Seek

354 *clean out of the way*: quite the wrong thing to do.
    Seek: Prefer.
355 *compassing*: achieving.
357 *fast*: true.

360 *hearted*: sincere, heart-felt.
361 *be conjunctive*: join together.

364 *delivered*: brought to birth.
    Traverse: About turn (a military term).

369 *betimes*: early.

376–98 Iago's soliloquy, where he plans the next moves in his campaign against Othello, uses the intimacy of verse and contrasts with the looser prose of the preceding lines.
376 *ever*: always.
    my fool my purse: make a profit out of a fool.
377 *gained knowledge*: experience.
    profane: abuse.
378 *expend*: waste.
    snipe: a marsh-bird, with a long beak.
379 *But*: Only.
380 *abroad*: generally.
    'twixt my sheets: in my bed.
381 *my office*: what I ought to do (i.e. he has slept with Iago's wife).
382 *for mere ... kind*: just because I suspect that sort of thing.
383 *do ... surety*: act as though I were certain.
    holds me well: thinks highly of me.
384 *purpose*: plan.

355 thou rather to be hanged in compassing thy joy than to be drowned and go without her.

Roderigo
Wilt thou be fast to my hopes, if I depend on the issue?

Iago
Thou art sure of me. Go make money. I have told thee often, and I re-tell thee again and again, I hate the
360 Moor. My cause is hearted: thine hath no less reason. Let us be conjunctive in our revenge against him. If thou canst cuckold him, thou dost thyself a pleasure, me a sport. There are many events in the womb of time, which will be delivered. Traverse! Go, provide
365 thy money. We will have more of this tomorrow. Adieu.

Roderigo
Where shall we meet i'th'morning?

Iago
At my lodging.

Roderigo
I'll be with thee betimes.

Iago
370 Go to; farewell. Do you hear, Roderigo?

Roderigo
What say you?

Iago
No more of drowning, do you hear?

Roderigo
I am changed.

Iago
Go to; farewell. Put money enough in your purse.

Roderigo
375 I'll sell all my land.   [*Exit*

Iago
Thus do I ever make my fool my purse:
For I mine own gained knowledge should profane
If I would time expend with such a snipe
But for my sport and profit. I hate the Moor,
380 And it is thought abroad that 'twixt my sheets
He's done my office. I know not if't be true
But I, for mere suspicion in that kind,
Will do as if for surety. He holds me well:
The better shall my purpose work on him.

385 *proper:* handsome.
   let me see now: We can see Iago's mind working.
386 *place:* job.
   plume up my will: give myself a bit of fun.
387 *double knavery:* i.e. tricking both Othello and Cassio.
388 *to abuse Othello's ear:* to deceive Othello by telling him.
389 *he:* i.e. Cassio.
390 *person:* agreeable appearance.
   smooth dispose: charming manner.
391 *To be suspected:* To arouse suspicion.
   framed: designed.
392 *free and open:* honest and trusting.
394 *tenderly:* easily.
   led by th'nose: fooled.
395 *asses:* The donkey's nose is sensitive, and only a slight pressure is needed to make the animal follow.
396 *engendered:* conceived.

385 Cassio's a proper man: let me see now;
To get his place and to plume up my will
In double knavery. How? How? Let's see.
After some time, to abuse Othello's ear
That he is too familiar with his wife;
390 He hath a person and a smooth dispose
To be suspected, framed to make women false.
The Moor is of a free and open nature,
That thinks men honest that but seem to be so,
And will as tenderly be led by th'nose
395 As asses are.
I have't. It is engendered. Hell and night
Must bring this monstrous birth to the world's light.
                                                    [*Exit*

Act 2

Act 2 Scene 1

In Cyprus, Montano and two gentlemen are
waiting for the arrival of Othello. There has
been a dreadful storm at sea; many of the
ships belonging to the Turkish enemy fleet
have been wrecked, but Cassio's ship has
landed safely. Cassio has no sooner given
the news of Othello's marriage when
Desdemona, accompanied by Iago and his
wife, also arrives in Cyprus. There is a
period of tension until Othello's ship comes
to land; Desdemona tries not to show her
anxiety, joking with Iago to distract her
mind. Eventually, however, the Moor and
his wife are re-united, and Othello describes
his great joy. The scene ends as Iago gives
further instructions to Roderigo, and at last
confides his plans for the audience to
hear—although the details are still unclear.

Scene 1

Enter Montano *and two* Gentlemen

Montano
What from the cape can you discern at sea?
First Gentleman
Nothing at all; it is a high-wrought flood.
I cannot 'twixt the heaven and the main
Descry a sail.
Montano
5 Methinks the wind does speak aloud at land;
A fuller blast ne'er shook our battlements.
If it hath ruffianed so upon the sea,
What ribs of oak, when mountains melt on them,
Can hold the mortise? What shall we hear of this?

2 *high-wrought flood*: tempestuous sea.
4 *Descry*: Detect.
5 *Methinks*: It seems to me.
6 *fuller*: more violent.
7 *ruffianed*: raged.
8 *ribs of oak*: wooden sides of a ship.
   mountains melt: mountainous waves cascade.
9 *hold the mortise*: hold together. A 'mortise'
   is a socket or joint.
   What ... this: What will come of this?
10 *segregation*: scattering.
11 *banning*: cursing.
12 *chidden billow*: waves which have been
   thrown back by the land.
   pelt: throw water on.
13 *wind-shaked surge*: wind-blown sea.
   main: might (some editions have 'mane',
   comparing the sea to a wild horse).
14 *burning Bear*: the constellation known as
   the Little Bear, two of whose brightest stars
   are called the 'Guardians' or *guards*.
15 *Pole*: The pole star, much used in
   navigation.
16 *like molestation*: such disturbance.
17 *enchafèd flood*: angry sea.
   If that: If.
18 *ensheltered and embayed*: sheltered in a bay.
19 *bear it out*: ride out the storm.
21 *banged*: beaten.
22 *designment halts*: their plans have been
   stopped.
23 *wrack*: shipwreck.
   sufferance: damage.
24 *On*: Of.
25 *put in*: anchored.
26 *A verinessa*: A cutter (a small single-masted
   vessel which, being much lighter than the
   warships which transport the other
   characters, would have less difficulty in
   coping with the storm).
28 *at sea*: is on the seas (i.e. on his way to
   Cyprus).
29 *in full commission*: in complete charge.
30 *a worthy governor*: this is high praise for
   Othello, since it comes from the man whose
   position he is taking.
32 *Touching*: With regard to.
   sadly: worried.
35 *served him*: served under him.
36 *full*: excellent.
38 *throw out our eyes*: look out.
39–40 *Even ... regard*: Until the sea and blue
   of the sky become indistinct to us.

Second Gentleman

10 A segregation of the Turkish fleet:
For do but stand upon the banning shore,
The chidden billow seems to pelt the clouds;
The wind-shaked surge, with high and monstrous
   main,
Seems to cast water on the burning Bear
15 And quench the guards of th'ever-fixèd Pole.
I never did like molestation view
On the enchafèd flood.

Montano   If that the Turkish fleet
Be not ensheltered and embayed, they are drowned:
It is impossible they bear it out.

Enter a Gentleman

Third Gentleman

20 News, lads! Our wars are done:
The desperate tempest hath so banged the Turks
That their designment halts. A noble ship of Venice
Hath seen a grievous wrack and sufferance
On most part of their fleet.

Montano

25 How! Is this true?

Third Gentleman   The ship is here put in,
A verinessa; Michael Cassio,
Lieutenant to the warlike Moor, Othello,
Is come on shore; the Moor himself at sea,
And is in full commission here for Cyprus.

Montano

30 I am glad on't; 'tis a worthy governor.

Third Gentleman

But this same Cassio, though he speak of comfort
Touching the Turkish loss, yet he looks sadly
And prays the Moor be safe; for they were parted
With foul and violent tempest.

Montano   Pray heaven he be:

35 For I have served him, and the man commands
Like a full soldier. Let's to the sea-side, ho!
As well to see the vessel that's come in,
As to throw out our eyes for brave Othello,
Even till we make the main and th'aerial blue
40 An indistinct regard.

42 *arrivance*: arrivals.

44 *so approve*: speak so well.

47 *Is ... shipped*: Does he have a good ship?

48 *bark*: vessel.
     stoutly timbered: well built (of wood).
49 *approved allowance*: tested experience.
50-51 *Therefore ... cure*: Cassio seems to be
     saying that he has never worried too much
     about Othello's safety, and he is now
     hopeful that all will be well.
52sd *within*: offstage.

53 *brow*: edge.
54 *ranks*: crowds.

55 I hope it is the governor.

56 *discharge ... courtesy*: fire a friendly shot.

58 *give us truth*: find out for certain.
60 *wived*: married.
61 *fortunately*: happily.
     achieved: won.
62 *paragons*: beats.
     fame: rumour.
63 *quirks*: fantasies.
     blazoning: describing; the word is
     particularly used in heraldry.
64 *essential ... creation*: in the perfect beauty
     of her created being.
65 *tire the ingener*: exhaust the designer (he
     has used up all his skill in perfecting
     Desdemona).

Third Gentleman   Come, let's do so;
For every minute is expectancy
Of more arrivance.

Enter Cassio

Cassio
Thanks, you the valiant of this warlike isle
That so approve the Moor! O, let the heavens
45 Give him defence against the elements,
For I have lost him on a dangerous sea.
Montano
Is he well-shipped?
Cassio
His bark is stoutly timbered, and his pilot
Of very expert and approved allowance;
50 Therefore my hopes, not surfeited to death,
Stand in bold cure.

[*Cry within* 'A sail, a sail, a sail!'

Cassio
What noise?
Fourth Gentleman
The town is empty; on the brow o'th'sea
Stand ranks of people, and they cry 'A sail!'
Cassio
55 My hopes do shape him for the governor.

[*A shot*]

Second Gentleman
They do discharge their shot of courtesy:
Our friends at least.
Cassio   I pray you, sir, go forth,
And give us truth who 'tis that is arrived.
Second Gentleman
I shall.   [*Exit*
Montano
60 But, good lieutenant, is your general wived?
Cassio
Most fortunately. He hath achieved a maid
That paragons description and wild fame;
One that excels the quirks of blazoning pens,
And in th'essential vesture of creation
65 Does tire the ingener.

69 *guttered*: splintered.
    congregated sands: sands heaped together
    (i.e. sandbanks).
70 *ensteeped*: submerged.
    guiltless: unwary.
    keel: ship.
71 *As having*: As though they had.
    sense: appreciation.
    omit: forget.
72 *mortal*: deadly.
73 *divine Desdemona*: This speech, building to
    a climax on the last line here, introduces
    Desdemona to Cyprus, heralding her arrival
    with a fanfare of verse just as the trumpet
    (at line 174) gives notice of Othello's
    arrival.
76 *footing*: landing.
    anticipates our thoughts: is sooner than we
    had expected.
77 *A se'nnight's speed*: A week (seven nights)
    early; Desdemona was to have been brought
    to Cyprus *after* Othello sailed from Venice.
    Jove: king of the gods of Roman
    mythology.
79 *bless ... ship*: the arrival of Othello would
    confer a blessing on the harbour.
    tall: handsome; Othello is sailing in the
    biggest of the three ships.
81 *extincted*: extinguished.
83 *riches*: i.e. Desdemona.
84 *have your knees*: bow to her—but there is
    the suggestion also of kneeling in prayer to
    the 'divine Desdemona'.
87 *Enwheel*: Encircle.
88 *tidings*: news.
89 *aught*: anything.

92 *contention*: battle.

Enter Second Gentleman

                        How now? Who has put in?
            Second Gentleman
    'Tis one Iago, ancient to the general.
            Cassio
    He's had most favourable and happy speed:
    Tempests themselves, high seas, and howling winds,
    The guttered rocks and congregated sands,
70 Traitors ensteeped to clog the guiltless keel,
    As having sense of beauty, do omit
    Their mortal natures, letting go safely by
    The divine Desdemona.
            Montano   What is she?
            Cassio
    She that I spake of, our great captain's captain,
75 Left in the conduct of the bold Iago,
    Whose footing here anticipates our thoughts
    A se'nnight's speed. Great Jove, Othello guard
    And swell his sail with thine own powerful breath,
    That he may bless this bay with his tall ship,
80 Make love's quick pants in Desdemona's arms,
    Give renewed fire to our extincted spirits,
    And bring all Cyprus comfort.

    Enter Desdemona, Emilia, Iago, Roderigo,
    and Attendants

                            O, behold,
    The riches of the ship is come on shore!
    You men of Cyprus, let her have your knees.
85 Hail to thee, lady! And the grace of heaven,
    Before, behind thee, and on every hand,
    Enwheel thee round.
            Desdemona   I thank you, valiant Cassio.
    What tidings can you tell me of my lord?
            Cassio
    He is not yet arrived; nor know I aught
90 But that he's well, and will be shortly here.
            Desdemona
    O but I fear! How lost you company?
            Cassio
    The great contention of the seas and skies
    Parted our fellowship.

93   *hark*: Cassio calls attention to the shout 'within'.

94   *their greeting*: the shots are being fired as a salvo, or friendly salute to the island (represented by its 'citadel').

95   *likewise*: the salute is friendly, so the ship must also be a friend.
  See for the news: Go to see what has happened.

97   *gall*: annoy.

98   *extend my manners*: show my respects (to Emilia).
  'Tis my breeding: I was brought up this way.

100–1   *so much ... me*: if she gave you her lips (in kissing) as much as she lets me hear her tongue (in talking).

103   *has no speech*: does not talk much.

104   *still*: always.
  have list: want.

105   *before your ladyship*: in your ladyship's presence.
  grant: admit.

106–7   She keeps her tongue to herself for a time, and only nags in her thoughts.

108–11   The quick drop into prose assures a relief of the audience's tension as it waits for Othello.

108   *pictures*: i.e. silent, unspeaking images.
  out of doors: in public.

109   *bells*: i.e. noisy, tongued instruments.
  parlours: at home.

109–10   *saints in your injuries*: sanctimonious when giving offence.
  being offended: when you are offended.
  players: actors, deceivers.

111   *housewifery*: housekeeping.
  housewives: hussies; Iago takes advantage of the word's semantic change.

112   *fie upon thee*: shame on you.

114   *rise to play*: i.e. at being good housekeepers.
  to work: i.e. as prostitutes.

[*Cry within* 'A sail, a sail!'
But hark, a sail!

[*A shot*]

Gentleman
They give their greeting to the citadel:
95   This likewise is a friend.
Cassio   See for the news.
                              [*Exit* Gentleman
Good ancient, you are welcome. Welcome, mistress.
Let it not gall your patience, good Iago,
That I extend my manners. 'Tis my breeding
That gives me this bold show of courtesy.

He kisses Emilia

Iago
100   Sir, would she give you so much of her lips
As of her tongue she oft bestows on me,
You'd have enough.
Desdemona
Alas, she has no speech.
Iago   In faith, too much.
I find it still when I have list to sleep.
105   Marry, before your ladyship, I grant
She puts her tongue a little in her heart
And chides with thinking.
Emilia   You have little cause to say so.
Iago
Come on, come on: you are pictures out of doors,
bells in your parlours, wild-cats in your kitchens, saints
110   in your injuries, devils being offended, players in your
housewifery, and housewives in your beds.
Desdemona
O fie upon thee, slanderer!
Iago
Nay, it is true, or else I am a Turk:
You rise to play and go to bed to work.
Emilia
115   You shall not write my praise.
Iago   No, let me not.
Desdemona
What wouldst thou write of me, if thou shouldst
  praise me?

117 *put me to't*: give me the task.

119 *assay*: make an attempt.
    one: someone; Desdemona's thoughts are
    not with Iago's foolery.

121 *beguile*: disguise.
122 *The thing I am*: i.e. worried.

125 *pate*: head.
    as ... frieze: i.e. a slow, sticky, process;
    lime was used to trap birds, and if it got on
    to fabric ('frieze' = a coarse woollen cloth)
    it was difficult to pull it off.
126 *my muse*: inspiration; the classical Muses
    were the goddesses responsible for artistic
    creation.
    labours: is struggling with it.
127 *is delivered*: has given birth.
130 *black*: brunette (as opposed to 'fair' =
    blonde).
    witty: clever.
132 *white*: Iago has a pun on 'wight' (= man).

135 *folly*: wantonness.

139 *thereunto*: as well.
143 *authority of her merit*: whose virtue
    deserves so much.

144 *put on the vouch*: compel the approval.
145–55 The couplets emphasize the triviality
    of Iago's thoughts.

Iago
O gentle lady, do not put me to't,
For I am nothing if not critical.
Desdemona
Come on, assay. There's one gone to the harbour?
Iago
120 Ay, madam.
Desdemona
[*Aside*] I am not merry, but I do beguile
The thing I am by seeming otherwise.
Come, how wouldst thou praise me?
Iago
I am about it, but indeed my invention
125 Comes from my pate as birdlime does from frieze—
It plucks out brains and all. But my muse labours,
And thus she is delivered:
If she be fair and wise, fairness and wit,
The one's for use, the other useth it.
Desdemona
130 Well praised! How if she be black and witty?
Iago
If she be black, and thereto have a wit,
She'll find a white that shall her blackness fit.
Desdemona
Worse and worse.
Emilia   How if fair and foolish?
Iago
She never yet was foolish that was fair,
135 For even her folly helped her to an heir.
Desdemona
These are old fond paradoxes to make fools laugh
i'th'alehouse. What miserable praise hast thou for her
that's foul and foolish?
Iago
There's none so foul and foolish thereunto,
140 But does foul pranks which fair and wise ones do.
Desdemona
O heavy ignorance! Thou praisest the worst best. But
what praise couldst thou bestow on a deserving woman
indeed? One that in the authority of her merit did
justly put on the vouch of very malice itself?

145 *ever*: always.
    fair: both 'beautiful' and 'virtuous'.
146 *Had tongue at will*: Could speak easily.
147 *gay*: garish.
148 Did not do as she wished, and yet knew she had power.
149 *her ... nigh*: when revenge was possible.
150 Accepted the injury and refused to be angry.
151 *frail*: Shakespeare uses this word frequently to refer to woman's sexual weakness; its presence suggests that 'the cod's head' and 'the salmon's tail' are intended with sexual overtones.
152 *cod*: a sea-fish; also a slang word for 'penis'.
    salmon's tail: a fish found in some British rivers; 'tail' is also a term for the sexual organs.
155 *wight*: person.
157 *chronicle small beer*: keep the household accounts.
158 *impotent*: feeble.
161 *liberal*: licentious.
162 *home*: plainly.
    relish: appreciate.
164 *takes her by the palm*: holds her hand.

    well said: well done.
165 *web*: spider's web.
166 *gyve*: fetter.
167 *courtship*: courtly behaviour.
168 *strip you out of*: lose your job for you.
170 *kissed ... fingers*: an Italian courtly gesture.
171 *apt*: ready.
    play the sir in: act the courtly gentleman.
173 *Would*: I wish.
    clyster-pipes: tubes for injecting an enema.
174 *his trumpet*: each commander had his own trumpet-call; Iago recognizes Othello's signal.

Iago
145 She that was ever fair and never proud,
    Had tongue at will, and yet was never loud;
    Never lacked gold, and yet went never gay;
    Fled from her wish, and yet said 'Now I may';
    She that being angered, her revenge being nigh,
150 Bade her wrong stay, and her displeasure fly;
    She that in wisdom never was so frail
    To change the cod's head for the salmon's tail;
    She that could think and ne'er disclose her mind:
    See suitors following and not look behind:
155 She was a wight, if ever such wight were—
Desdemona
To do what?
Iago
To suckle fools and chronicle small beer.
Desdemona
O, most lame and impotent conclusion!
Do not learn of him, Emilia, though he be thy
160 husband. How say you, Cassio, is he not a most
profane and liberal counsellor?
Cassio
He speaks home, madam; you may relish him more in
the soldier than in the scholar.
Iago
[*Aside*] He takes her by the palm. Ay, well said,
165 whisper. With as little a web as this will I ensnare as
great a fly as Cassio. Ay, smile upon her, do. I will gyve
thee in thine own courtship. You say true, 'tis so
indeed. If such tricks as these strip you out of your
lieutenantry, it had been better you had not
170 kissed your three fingers so oft, which now again you
are most apt to play the sir in. Very good: well kissed,
an excellent courtesy! 'Tis so indeed. Yet again your
fingers to your lips? Would they were clyster-pipes for
your sake!
        [*Trumpet*]
[*Aloud*] The Moor! I know his trumpet.
Cassio   'Tis truly so.
Desdemona
175 Let's meet him and receive him.
Cassio   Lo where he comes!

Enter Othello *and* Attendants

176   The greetings of Othello and Desdemona initiate one of the great moments in the play; for a few lines all the other characters, and the business of war, are forgotten as the two lovers share in the bliss of their re-union.

181   *labouring bark*: struggling ship.
182   *Olympus-high*: As high as Mount Olympus, home of the gods in classical mythology.
      duck: dive down.
183   *it were now to die*: I were to die now.
185   *content*: happiness.
      absolute: perfect.
187   *Succeeds*: Follows.
      unknown fate: the life to come.

189   *as ... grow*: as long as our lives last.
      Amen: Othello responds to Desdemona's prayer.
191   *stops me here*: chokes me.
192   *this*: i.e. the kiss.
      be: may be.
193   Iago picks up and continues Othello's musical imagery.
194   *set down the pegs*: loosen the screws (thereby slackening the strings of a musical instrument like the lute).
197   *my old acquaintance*: the people I used to know; after the intense moment of joy, Othello turns to the everyday world of common good manners, recognizing the existence of other people again.
198   *Honey*: A term of affection for Desdemona.
      well desired: well received.
200   *I prattle ... fashion*: I shouldn't be talking like this.
200–1 *I dote ... comforts*: Othello has so much good news to impart that he cannot speak sensibly.
202   *disembark my coffers*: unload my luggage.
203   *master*: i.e. of the ship.

205   *challenge*: demand.

Othello
O my fair warrior!
        Desdemona   My dear Othello!
        Othello
It gives me wonder great as my content
To see you here before me. O my soul's joy!
If after every tempest come such calms,
180 May the winds blow till they have wakened death,
And let the labouring bark climb hills of seas
Olympus-high, and duck again as low
As hell's from heaven. If it were now to die,
'Twere now to be most happy; for I fear
185 My soul hath her content so absolute
That not another comfort like to this
Succeeds in unknown fate.
        Desdemona   The heavens forbid
But that our loves and comforts should increase,
Even as our days do grow.
        Othello   Amen to that, sweet Powers!
190 I cannot speak enough of this content;
It stops me here; it is too much of joy.

                                        [*They kiss*

And this, and this the greatest discords be
That e'er our hearts shall make.
        Iago [*Aside*]   O, you are well tuned now!
But I'll set down the pegs that make this music,
195 As honest as I am.
        Othello   Come, let us to the castle.
News, friends; our wars are done; the Turks are
    drowned.
How does my old acquaintance of this isle?
Honey, you shall be well desired in Cyprus:
I have found great love amongst them. O my sweet,
200 I prattle out of fashion, and I dote
In mine own comforts. I prithee, good Iago,
Go to the bay and disembark my coffers;
Bring thou the master to the citadel;
He is a good one, and his worthiness
205 Does challenge much respect. Come, Desdemona,
Once more well met at Cyprus!
                        [*Exeunt all except* Iago *and* Roderigo

207 *presently*: immediately.
210 *is native to them*: they are born with.
211 *list*: listen.
     watches: keeps the night watch.
212 *court of guard*: guard-room.
213 *directly*: definitely.
215 *Lay ... thus*: Put your finger on your lips:
     i.e. keep quiet.
     thy soul: yourself.
216 *Mark me*: Remember.
217 *but*: only.
218 *love him still*: continue to love him.
     prating: boasting.
     discreet heart: commonsense.
219 *fed*: satisfied.
220 *the devil*: Othello's blackness identifies
     him (for Iago) as the devil.
     the blood: passion.
221 *act of sport*: sexual intercourse.
222 *to inflame it*: to arouse desire.
     give ... appetite: further stimulation to
     desire that is already satisfied.
223 *favour*: appearance.
     sympathy in years: agreement in age.
     manners: culture.
225 *required conveniences*: necessary
     qualifications.
226 *heave the gorge*: feel sick.
227 *disrelish*: lose her taste for.
     Very nature: Her own nature.
229 *pregnant ... position*: obvious and natural
     assumption.
230-1 *who stands ... fortune*: who is so well
     placed to be next to receive this fortune.
232 *voluble*: smooth-tongued.
     no further conscionable: with no more
     conscience.
233 *mere form ... seeming*: only the outward
     appearance of good manners and sensitivity.
234 *compassing*: achieving.
     salt: lecherous.
     loose affection: immoral desires.
235 *slipper*: slippery.
236 *finder out of occasions*: one who will take
     every opportunity.
237 *stamp and counterfeit advantages*: forge
     false advantage (as though he were forging
     coins).
240 *green*: young, unripe.
     look after: want.
242 *found*: recognized his nature and
     intentions.
243 *blessed condition*: innocence.

Iago

[*To soldiers, who go off*] Do thou meet me presently at the harbour. [*To* Roderigo] Come hither. If thou be'st valiant—as they say base men being in love have then a nobility in their natures more than is native to them—list me. The lieutenant tonight watches on the court of guard. First, I must tell thee this: Desdemona is directly in love with him.

Roderigo

With him? Why, 'tis not possible!

Iago

Lay thy finger thus, and let thy soul be instructed. Mark me with what violence she first loved the Moor, but for bragging and telling her fantastical lies. And will she love him still for prating? Let not thy discreet heart think it. Her eye must be fed. And what delight shall she have to look on the devil? When the blood is made dull with the act of sport, there should be, again to inflame it and give satiety a fresh appetite, loveliness in favour, sympathy in years, manners and beauties: all which the Moor is defective in. Now for want of these required conveniences, her delicate tenderness will find itself abused, begin to heave the gorge, disrelish and abhor the Moor. Very nature will instruct her in it and compel her to some second choice. Now, sir, this granted—as it is a most pregnant and unforced position—who stands so eminently in the degree of this fortune as Cassio does?—a knave very voluble; no further conscionable than in putting on the mere form of civil and humane seeming for the better compassing of his salt and most hidden loose affection. Why, none; why, none—a slipper and subtle knave, a finder out of occasions; that has an eye can stamp and counterfeit advantages, though true advantage never present itself; a devilish knave! Besides, the knave is handsome, young, and hath all those requisites in him that folly and green minds look after. A pestilent complete knave; and the woman hath found him already.

Roderigo

I cannot believe that in her: she's full of most blessed condition.

244 *fig's end*: rubbish; the exclamation would
      be accompanied with an obscene gesture.
244–5 *The wine ... grapes*: i.e. she's only
      human.
246 *pudding*: nonsense.
247 *paddle with*: caress.

250 *index ... prologue*: like the index to a book,
      it shows what is to come, but the
      introduction to the book cannot
      immediately be understood.
252 *near*: close.
254 *mutualities*: intimacies.
      marshal: lead.
      hard at hand: close behind.
255 *incorporate*: bodily.
256 *be ... me*: do as I shall tell you.
257 *Watch*: Keep guard (as Cassio will be
      doing).
257–8 *for ... you*: I'll give you your
      instructions.
260 *tainting*: questioning.
262 *minister*: provide.

264 *sudden*: quick to act.
      in choler: when he's angry.
      haply: perhaps.
266 *even out of that*: for that reason.
267 *qualification*: pacifying.
268 *displanting*: dismissal.

270 *prefer*: promote.
271 *profitably*: usefully.

273 *prosperity*: success.

275 *warrant*: promise.
      by and by: shortly.
276 *his necessaries*: Othello's luggage.

Iago
Blessed fig's end! The wine she drinks is made of
245 grapes. If she had been blessed, she would never have
loved the Moor. Blessed pudding! Didst thou not see
her paddle with the palm of his hand? Didst not mark
that?

Roderigo
Yes, that I did: but that was but courtesy.

Iago
250 Lechery, by this hand: an index and obscure
prologue to the history of lust and foul thoughts. They
met so near with their lips that their breaths embraced
together. Villainous thoughts, Roderigo! When these
mutualities so marshal the way, hard at hand comes the
255 master and main exercise, th'incorporate conclusion.
Pish! But, sir, be you ruled by me. I have brought you
from Venice. Watch you tonight: for the command, I'll
lay't upon you. Cassio knows you not; I'll not be far
from you. Do you find some occasion to anger Cassio,
260 either by speaking too loud, or tainting his discipline,
or from what other course you please, which the time
shall more favourably minister.

Roderigo
Well.

Iago
Sir, he's rash and very sudden in choler, and haply
265 with his truncheon may strike at you: provoke
him that he may, for even out of that will I cause these
of Cyprus to mutiny, whose qualification shall come
into no true taste again but by the displanting of
Cassio. So shall you have a shorter journey to your
270 desires by the means I shall then have to prefer them,
and the impediment most profitably removed,
without the which there were no expectation of our
prosperity.

Roderigo
I will do this, if you can bring it to any opportunity.

Iago
275 I warrant thee. Meet me by and by at the citadel. I
must fetch his necessaries ashore. Farewell.

Roderigo
Adieu.   [*Exit*

278–304 Iago's soliloquy, as usual, is in verse; he is thinking aloud, and the audience is able to over-hear his thoughts.

279 *apt and of great credit*: likely, and could well be believed.

280 *howbeit*: although; even Iago must confess Othello's nobility.

283 *dear*: not only 'loving' and 'beloved', but also 'costly'.

284 *not ... lust*: not simply for lust.
peradventure: perhaps.

285 *accountant*: accountable.

286 *diet*: feed.

287 *lusty*: lustful.

288 *leaped into my seat*: i.e. made love to Emilia.

289 *inwards*: guts.

291 *evened*: get even.

295 *trash*: rubbish.
leash: The readings of both Quarto ('crush') and Folio ('trace') are difficult; 'leash' is an emendation first suggested by Dover Wilson. Iago seems to be saying that he is using Roderigo like a hound to force Cassio into an awkward situation.

296 *stand ... on*: will do what I want.

297 *on the hip*: at my mercy; the hip, or haunch, of the deer is the part usually grabbed by the hunting hounds.

298 *Abuse*: Slander.
the rank garb: a foul manner—by accusing him of adultery.

299 *with my nightcap*: i.e. in bed with Emilia.

301 *egregiously*: extraordinarily.

302 *practising upon*: plotting against.

303 *Even to madness*: To drive him mad.
'Tis here: i.e. the plot is in Iago's mind already.

Act 2 Scene 2

A Herald reads Othello's proclamation to the citizens of Cyprus: there is to be general rejoicing, to celebrate the end of the Turkish threat to the island, and also to honour the marriage of Desdemona and Othello. The short scene reminds us of the situation in Cyprus: it is an island newly released from the threat of war.

2 *certain tidings*: definite information.

3 *mere perdition*: total destruction.

4 *put himself into*: enjoy.
triumph: celebration.

6 *addiction*: pleasure.

7 *nuptial*: marriage.

Iago

That Cassio loves her, I do well believe't:
That she loves him, 'tis apt and of great credit.
280 The Moor—howbeit that I endure him not—
Is of a constant, loving, noble nature,
And, I dare think, he'll prove to Desdemona
A most dear husband. Now, I do love her too;
Not out of absolute lust—though peradventure
285 I stand accountant for as great a sin—
But partly led to diet my revenge
For that I do suspect the lusty Moor
Hath leaped into my seat, the thought whereof
Doth, like a poisonous mineral, gnaw my inwards,
290 And nothing can, or shall, content my soul
Till I am evened with him, wife for wife;
Or failing so, yet that I put the Moor
At least into a jealousy so strong
That judgement cannot cure. Which thing to do
295 If this poor trash of Venice, whom I leash
For his quick hunting, stand the putting on,
I'll have our Michael Cassio on the hip,
Abuse him to the Moor in the rank garb—
For I fear Cassio with my night-cap too—
300 Make the Moor thank me, love me, and reward me
For making him egregiously an ass,
And practising upon his peace and quiet,
Even to madness. 'Tis here, but yet confused:
Knavery's plain face is never seen till used.   [*Exit*

Scene 2

Enter Herald, *with a proclamation*

Herald

It is Othello's pleasure, our noble and valiant general,
that upon certain tidings now arrived importing the
mere perdition of the Turkish fleet, every man put
himself into triumph: some to dance, some to
5 make bonfires, each man to what sport and revels his
addiction leads him. For, besides these beneficial news,
it is the celebration of his nuptial. So much was his
pleasure should be proclaimed. All offices are open,
and there is full liberty of feasting from this

8 *offices*: stores (catering for food and drink).
9 *full liberty of feasting*: all feasting is free.
10 *bell*: curfew bell.
    told: struck (an alternative spelling would
    be 'tolled').

Act 2   Scene 3

Othello and Desdemona withdraw from the
general revelry, but Iago persuades Cassio
that there is time for one more drink.
Another drink proves too much for Cassio,
who has already declared his inability to
cope with liquor; and when Roderigo (on
Iago's instructions) offends him, Cassio
starts a fight. Montano, the governor of
Cyprus is hurt. Othello is roused, and when
he hears Iago's version of the affair, he
dismisses Cassio from his military post.
Cassio confides his grief to Iago, and is
advised to seek Desdemona's assistance.
Roderigo is angry about the way he has
been beaten, and he threatens to return to
Venice. But Iago convinces him that
everything is under control.

1   *Michael*: Othello's tone is relaxed, and he
    uses Cassio's Christian name as a sign of
    friendship.
    look you: you take care of.
2   *stop*: restraint.
3   *outsport discretion*: enjoy ourselves more
    than is wise.
4   *hath ... to do*: knows what to do.
5–6 Although Iago knows the job, he still
    needs the supervision of a senior officer;
    these lines are a reminder that Cassio is in
    fact Iago's superior.
6   *honest*: This word, which is capable of a
    variety of meanings, is always associated
    with Iago: eventually it has a deadly irony.
    Here it is used simply to mean 'reliable'.
7   *with your earliest*: as soon as you can.
9–10 The marriage has been celebrated, but
    not yet consummated.
12 *to*: go to.
13 *this hour*: for another hour.
14 *cast*: dismissed.
15 *who ... blame*: and who can blame him.
16 *made wanton the night*: enjoyed the pleasure
    of the night.
17 *sport for Jove*: Jove, king of the classical
    gods was famous for his sexual adventures.
19 *full of game*: sexually responsive.

10 present hour of five till the bell have told eleven.
    Heaven bless the isle of Cyprus and our noble general
    Othello!   [*Exit*

Scene 3

> *Enter* Othello, Desdemona, Cassio, *and*
> Attendants

Othello
Good Michael, look you to the guard tonight.
Let's teach ourselves that honourable stop,
Not to outsport discretion.
    Cassio
Iago hath direction what to do;
5 But, notwithstanding, with my personal eye
Will I look to't.
    Othello   Iago is most honest.
Michael, good night. Tomorrow with your earliest
Let me have speech with you. [*To* Desdemona]
    Come, my dear love,
The purchase made, the fruits are to ensue:
10 That profit's yet to come 'tween me and you.
Good night.
    [*Exeunt* Othello, Desdemona, *and* Attendants

> *Enter* Iago

    Cassio
Welcome Iago; we must to the watch.
    Iago
Not this hour, lieutenant; 'tis not yet ten o'th'clock.
Our general cast us thus early for the love of
15 his Desdemona; who let us not therefore blame. He
hath not yet made wanton the night with her; and she
is sport for Jove.
    Cassio
She is a most exquisite lady.
    Iago
And, I'll warrant her, full of game.
    Cassio
20 Indeed, she is a most fresh and delicate creature.

21 *sounds a parley*: sends out a summons (as a trumpet might call military commanders to come together).

23 *right*: very.
24 *alarum*: waking call (sounded on the trumpet for soldiers).

27 *stoup*: jug.
    here without: just outside.
    brace: pair.
28 *gallants*: good chaps.
    fain: like to.
    have a measure: drink a toast.
30-31 *poor ... brains*: a very poor head (i.e. he is quickly intoxicated).
33 *I'll ... you*: I'll drink in your place (to distract attention from the fact that Cassio is not drinking).

35-6 *craftily qualified*: cunningly mixed.
    innovation: alteration.
37 *here*: in his head.

43 *it dislikes me*: I don't like it.
44 *fasten ... him*: get him to have just one more drink; Iago moves into verse for this moment of self-revelation.
46 *full ... offence*: ready to take and give offence.
47 *my ... dog*: any girl's pet dog; no specific 'mistress' is intended.
    sick: stupid.
48 *turned ... out*: almost transformed.
49 *To Desdemona*: To Desdemona's health.
    caroused: drunk.
50 *Potations*: drinks.
    pottle-deep: whole pottles full (a 'pottle' held about two litres).
    to watch: to go on guard (although Roderigo is a civilian).

Iago
What an eye she has! Methinks it sounds a parley to provocation.
Cassio
An inviting eye, and yet methinks right modest.
Iago
And when she speaks, is it not an alarum to love?
Cassio
25 She is indeed perfection.
Iago
Well, happiness to their sheets! Come, lieutenant, I have a stoup of wine; and here without are a brace of Cyprus gallants that would fain have a measure to the health of black Othello.
Cassio
30 Not tonight, good Iago. I have very poor and unhappy brains for drinking. I could well wish courtesy would invent some other custom of entertainment.
Iago
O, they are our friends! But one cup; I'll drink for you.
Cassio
35 I have drunk but one cup tonight, and that was craftily qualified too; and behold what innovation it makes here. I am unfortunate in the infirmity and dare not task my weakness with any more.
Iago
What, man! 'Tis a night of revels; the gallants 40 desire it.
Cassio
Where are they?
Iago
Here, at the door: I pray you call them in.
Cassio
I'll do't, but it dislikes me.   [*Exit*
Iago
If I can fasten but one cup upon him,
45 With that which he hath drunk tonight already,
He'll be as full of quarrel and offence
As my young mistress' dog. Now my sick fool Roderigo,
Whom love hath turned almost the wrong side out,
To Desdemona hath tonight caroused
50 Potations pottle-deep; and he's to watch.

51	*else*: others.
	noble swelling spirits: high-spirited.
52	Who are quick to take offence when they suspect an insult to their honour.
53	*very elements*: truly typical.
	warlike: prepared for war.
54	*flustered*: confused.
	flowing: over-flowing.
55	*watch*: are on guard.
56	*action*: quarrel.
57	*offend the isle*: cause some disturbance to the island.
58	*consequence*: what happens next.
	approve: bear out, confirm.
	dream: scheme.
59	Everything is going well.
60	*'Fore God*: I swear before God.
	rouse: drink.
61	*past*: more than.
64	*canakin*: little can.
67	*span*: short time.
68	*let a soldier drink*: Iago chose his song wisely.
72	*potent in potting*: heavy drinkers.
	Your: This word is used simply for colloquial emphasis—and so is 'you' in line 76.
73	*swag-bellied*: with a sagging belly.
	drink, ho: Iago calls for more wine.
76	*with facility*: easily.
77	*sweats not*: finds it no effort.
	Almaine: German.
78	*gives ... vomit*: makes the Dutchman sick.

Three else of Cyprus, noble swelling spirits—
That hold their honours in a wary distance,
The very elements of this warlike isle—
Have I tonight flustered with flowing cups,
55 And they watch too. Now 'mongst this flock of drunkards,
Am I to put our Cassio in some action
That may offend the isle. But here they come;
If consequence do but approve my dream,
My boat sails freely both with wind and stream.

Enter Cassio *with* Montano *and*
Gentlemen, *and* Servants *with wine*

Cassio
60 'Fore God, they have given me a rouse already.
Montano
Good faith, a little one; not past a pint, as I am a
soldier.
Iago
Some wine, ho!
  [*Sings*]   And let me the canakin clink, clink;
65   And let me the canakin clink;
            A soldier's a man
            A man's life's but a span;
            Why, then, let a soldier drink.
Some wine, boys.
Cassio
70 'Fore God, an excellent song.
Iago
I learned it in England, where indeed they are most
potent in potting. Your Dane, your Germans, and your
swag-bellied Hollander—drink, ho!—are nothing to
your English.
Cassio
75 Is your Englishman so expert in his drinking?
Iago
Why, he drinks you with facility your Dane dead
drunk; he sweats not to overthrow your Almaine; he
gives your Hollander a vomit, ere the next pottle can be
filled.
Cassio
80 To the health of our general!
Montano
I am for it, lieutenant; and I'll do you justice.

83 *and-a*: two syllables added to the line for rhythm, not sense.
84 *a crown*: a unit of money; the coin was so called because a crown was stamped on it.
85 He thought that was sixpence too much.
86 *lown*: rascal.

90 *auld*: old (the form of the word probably indicates that the ballad comes from the north of England).

95–110 Cassio's words merely indicate the state of his drunkenness.

104 *before the ancient*: Cassio's drunken remark will heighten Iago's jealousy.

114 *platform*: a level place for mounting artillery.
set the watch: mount the guard. Montano gives the instruction because Cassio—now very drunk—has forgotten to do so.

Iago
O, sweet England!
   [*Sings*]   King Stephen was and-a worthy peer,
         His breeches cost him but a crown;
      He held them sixpence all too dear;
         With that he called the tailor lown,
      He was a wight of high renown,
         And thou art but of low degree;
      'Tis pride that pulls the country down;
85
90
         Then take thine auld cloak about thee.
Some wine, ho!
Cassio
'Fore God, this is a more exquisite song than the other.
Iago
Will you hear't again?
Cassio
95 No, for I hold him to be unworthy of his place that does those things. Well, God's above all; and there be souls must be saved, and there be souls must not be saved.
Iago
It's true, good lieutenant.
Cassio
100 For mine own part—no offence to the general, nor any man of quality—I hope to be saved.
Iago
And so do I too, lieutenant.
Cassio
Ay, but, by your leave, not before me. The lieutenant is to be saved before the ancient. Let's have no
105 more of this; let's to our affairs. God forgive us our sins. Gentlemen, let's look to our business. Do not think, gentlemen, I am drunk: this is my ancient, this is my right hand, and this is my left. I am not drunk now: I can stand well enough and I speak well
110 enough.
Gentlemen
Excellent well.
Cassio
Why, very well; you must not think then that I am drunk.   [*Exit*
Montano
To th'platform, masters; come, let's set the watch.

115   *before*: ahead; Iago loses no opportunity
      for slandering Cassio.
116   *Caesar*: The great Roman conqueror.
118   *just equinox*: exact equivalent.

121   *odd time*: occasion.
122   *shake*: ruin.
123   He's always like this before he goes to
      sleep.
124   He'll stay awake while the clock
      ('horologe') goes round a couple of times (a
      'double set').
125   *rock not his cradle*: doesn't put him to
      sleep.
126   *put in mind*: made aware; Montano is
      worried about the island's security.

133   *hazard*: risk.
134   *ingraft*: rooted.

142   *twiggen-bottle*: a bottle encased with
      wicker-work; Cassio probably threatens to
      beat Roderigo until he goes through the
      basketwork and into the bottle.

Iago

115 You see this fellow that is gone before;
He is a soldier, fit to stand by Caesar
And give direction; and do but see his vice:
'Tis to his virtue a just equinox,
The one as long as th'other. 'Tis pity of him.

120 I fear the trust Othello puts in him,
On some odd time of his infirmity,
Will shake this island.

Montano   But is he often thus?

Iago
'Tis evermore the prologue to his sleep:
He'll watch the horologe a double set,

125 If drink rock not his cradle.

Montano   It were well
The general were put in mind of it:
Perhaps he sees it not, or his good nature
Prizes the virtue that appears in Cassio
And looks not on his evils. Is not this true?

Enter Roderigo

Iago
130 [*Aside*] How now, Roderigo!
I pray you after the lieutenant go!   [*Exit* Roderigo

Montano
And 'tis great pity that the noble Moor
Should hazard such a place as his own second
With one of an ingraft infirmity.

135 It were an honest action to say
So to the Moor.

Iago   Not I, for this fair island!
I do love Cassio well and would do much
To cure him of this evil.

                          [*Cry within* 'Help! Help!']
                          But hark what noise?

Enter Cassio, *pursuing* Roderigo

Cassio
Zounds, you rogue, you rascal!

Montano
140 What's the matter, lieutenant?

Cassio
A knave teach me my duty? I'll beat the knave into a
twiggen-bottle.

Roderigo
Beat me?
Cassio
Dost thou prate, rogue?

He strikes Roderigo

Montano
145 Nay, good lieutenant; I pray you, sir, hold your
hand.

147 *mazzard*: head.

Cassio
Let me go, sir, or I'll knock you o'er the mazzard.
Montano
Come, come, you're drunk.
Cassio
Drunk!
Iago

150 *cry a mutiny*: tell everyone that there is a riot.
151 *God's will*: let God's will be done; Iago calls for peace.

150 [*To* Roderigo] Away, I say; go out and cry a mutiny.
                              [*Exit* Roderigo
Nay, good lieutenant. God's will, gentlemen!
Help, ho! lieutenant! Sir! Montano! Sir!
Help, masters. Here's a goodly watch indeed.

[*Bell rings*]

154 *Diablo*: Iago uses the Spanish exclamation (= the devil).
155 *town*: all the citizens.

Who's that which rings the bell? Diablo, ho!
155 The town will rise. God's will, lieutenant, hold!
You will be shamed for ever!

Enter Othello *and* Attendants

Othello
What is the matter here?
Montano   Zounds, I bleed still.

158 *hurt to th'death*: fatally wounded.
    Hold: Stop.
163 *Are we turned*: Have we become?
164 *forbid*: heaven refused to let the Ottomites fight the Venetians by sending the storm to wreck the Turkish fleet.
165 *put by*: cease.
    barbarous: i.e. fighting as though they were barbarians (like the Turks).
166 *stirs*: moves.
    to carve: to cut meat—i.e. to stab someone.
    for his own rage: to satisfy his anger (one might 'carve' meat to satisfy hunger).
167 *Holds ... light*: Has little care for his life.
    upon his motion: as soon as he moves.

I am hurt to th'death.
Othello   Hold for your lives!
Iago
Hold, ho, lieutenant, sir, Montano, gentlemen!
160 Have you forgot all sense of place and duty?
Hold! The general speaks to you: hold, for shame!
Othello
Why, how now, ho! From whence ariseth this?
Are we turned Turks and to ourselves do that
Which heaven hath forbid the Ottomites?
165 For Christian shame, put by this barbarous brawl.
He that stirs next to carve for his own rage
Holds his soul light: he dies upon his motion.

169 *propriety*: normal peaceful state.
170 *grieving*: distress.
171 *On thy love*: On your loyalty.
     I charge thee: I order you to speak.
172 *Friends all but now*: Just now we were all
     friends.
     even now: only just now.
173 *quarter*: closeness.
     terms: friendship.
174 *Devesting them*: Undressing themselves.
175 *unwitted men*: driven them insane; it was
     thought that planets (especially the moon)
     had influence over men's mind.
176 *tilting*: striking.
177 *opposition bloody*: fighting with bloodshed.
177–8 *I cannot ... beginning*: I cannot tell you
     how it started.
178 *peevish odds*: nasty quarrel.
179 *would*: I wish.
     action: battle.
181 *are thus forgot*: have forgotten yourself like
     this.
183 *you ... civil*: you used to be law-abiding.
184 *stillness*: peacefulness.

186 *censure*: judgement.
187 *unlace*: unloosen.
188 *spend your rich opinion*: exchange your
     good reputation.
     for the name: to be called.
189 *night-brawler*: night-fighter.

190 *hurt to danger*: seriously injured.

192 *spare*: save.
     which ... me: which now hurts a bit.

194 *amiss*: wrong.
195 *self-charity*: self-protection.

197 *assails*: attacks.

198 *blood*: temper.
     safer guides: i.e. reason.
199 *collied*: blackened.
200 *Assays*: Attempts.

203 *rout*: uproar.
     set it on: started it.

Silence that dreadful bell: it frights the isle
From her propriety. What is the matter, masters?
170 Honest Iago, that looks dead with grieving,
Speak, who began this? On thy love I charge thee.
          Iago
I do not know. Friends all but now, even now,
In quarter and in terms like bride and groom
Devesting them for bed: and then but now—
175 As if some planet had unwitted men—
Swords out, and tilting one at other's breasts
In opposition bloody. I cannot speak
Any beginning to this peevish odds;
And would in action glorious I had lost
180 Those legs that brought me to a part of it.
          Othello
How comes it, Michael, you are thus forgot?
          Cassio
I pray you pardon me: I cannot speak.
          Othello
Worthy Montano, you were wont to be civil:
The gravity and stillness of your youth
185 The world hath noted; and your name is great
In mouths of wisest censure. What's the matter
That you unlace your reputation thus
And spend your rich opinion for the name
Of a night-brawler? Give me answer to it.
          Montano
190 Worthy Othello, I am hurt to danger.
Your officer, Iago, can inform you,
While I spare speech, which something now offends
     me,
Of all that I do know; nor know I aught
By me that's said or done amiss this night,
195 Unless self-charity be sometimes a vice,
And to defend ourselves it be a sin
When violence assails us.
          Othello   Now, by heaven,
My blood begins my safer guides to rule,
And passion, having my best judgement collied,
200 Assays to lead the way. Zounds, if I stir,
Or do but lift this arm, the best of you
Shall sink in my rebuke. Give me to know
How this foul rout began, who set it on;

204 *approved*: found guilty.
205 *Though ... me*: Even if he were my twin-brother.
206-7 *a town ... wild*: a town still in a state of panic because of the war.
208 *manage*: conduct.

211 *partially affined*: taking sides.
   leagued in office: loyalty to a superior.

213 *Touch ... near*: Don't make things more difficult.

220 *determined*: drawn.
221 *To ... him*: To strike him.
   this gentleman: i.e. Montano.
222 *Steps in*: Goes up to.
   entreats his pause: begs him to stop.
223 *Myself*: I myself.
   the crying fellow: i.e. Roderigo.
224 *as it so fell out*: which was what happened.
225 *fall in fright*: be alarmed.
226 *Outran my purpose*: Ran faster than I thought.
226-7 *I returned ... For that*: I thought it better to come back because.
228 *high in oath*: swearing loudly.
230 *close*: fighting.
231 *At*: With.

238 *indignity*: insult.
239 *pass*: ignore.

240 *mince*: tone down.
241 *Making ... Cassio*: Making light of Cassio's part in the fight.

And he that is approved in this offence,
205 Though he had twinned with me, both at a birth,
Shall lose me. What! In a town of war
Yet wild, the people's hearts brimful of fear,
To manage private and domestic quarrel
In night, and on the court and guard of safety,
210 'Tis monstrous. Iago, who began't?
   Montano
If partially affined or leagued in office,
Thou dost deliver more or less than truth,
Thou art no soldier.
   Iago   Touch me not so near.
I had rather have this tongue cut from my mouth
215 Than it should do offence to Michael Cassio.
Yet, I persuade myself, to speak the truth
Shall nothing wrong him. This it is, general.
Montano and myself being in speech,
There comes a fellow, crying out for help,
220 And Cassio following with determined sword
To execute upon him. Sir, this gentleman
Steps in to Cassio and entreats his pause:
Myself the crying fellow did pursue
Lest by his clamour—as it so fell out—
225 The town might fall in fright. He, swift of foot,
Outran my purpose and I returned the rather
For that I heard the clink and fall of swords
And Cassio high in oath, which till tonight
I ne'er might say before. When I came back—
230 For this was brief—I found them close together
At blow and thrust, even as again they were
When you yourself did part them.
More of this matter can I not report:
But men are men; the best sometimes forget.
235 Though Cassio did some little wrong to him,
As men in rage strike those that wish them best,
Yet surely Cassio, I believe, received
From him that fled some strange indignity
Which patience could not pass.
   Othello   I know, Iago,
240 Thy honesty and love doth mince this matter,
Making it light to Cassio. Cassio, I love thee,
But nevermore be officer of mine.

Enter Desdemona, *attended*

Look if my gentle love be not raised up.
I'll make thee an example.

Desdemona   What is the matter, dear?

Othello

245 All's well now, sweeting: come away to bed.
Sir, for your hurts, myself will be your surgeon.
                    [Montano *is led off*
Iago, look with care about the town
And silence those whom this vile brawl distracted.
Come, Desdemona, 'tis the soldiers' life

250 To have their balmy slumbers waked with strife.
                    [*Exeunt all but* Iago *and* Cassio

Iago

What, are you hurt, lieutenant?

Cassio

Ay, past all surgery.

Iago

Marry, God forbid!

Cassio

Reputation, reputation, reputation! O, I have lost my
255 reputation! I have lost the immortal part of myself, and
what remains is bestial. My reputation, Iago, my
reputation!

Iago

As I am an honest man I thought you had received
some bodily wound: there is more of sense in that than
260 in reputation. Reputation is an idle and most false
imposition; oft got without merit and lost without
deserving. You have lost no reputation at all, unless
you repute yourself such a loser. What, man! There are
ways to recover the general again. You are but now cast
265 in his mood—a punishment more in policy than in
malice—even so as one would beat his offenceless dog
to affright an imperious lion. Sue to him again, and
he's yours.

Cassio

I will rather sue to be despised than to deceive so good
270 a commander with so slight, so drunken, and so
indiscreet an officer. Drunk! And speak parrot! And
squabble! Swagger! Swear! And discourse fustian with
one's own shadow! O, thou invisible spirit of

---

243 *raised up*: disturbed.
244 The dismissal of Cassio will show the rest
of the army, and the islanders, that Othello
will not tolerate disorderly conduct.

246 *hurts*: wounds.
myself ... surgeon: I will pay for your
surgeon myself.

248 *distracted*: disturbed.

252 *past all surgery*: beyond medical help; the
change from verse to prose signals a change
in the mood and pace of the scene.

259 *of sense*: feeling.

261 *imposition*: burden.

263 *repute*: consider.
264 *recover the general*: win back Othello's
friendship.
264-5 *You ... mood*: You have only been
dismissed because of his temper.
265 *in policy*: for political reasons.
266 *malice*: ill-will.
266-7 Just as one might punish the innocent
as a deterrent to the real criminal; the
expression is proverbial.
267 *Sue*: Appeal.
271 *speak parrot*: talk nonsense.
272 *fustian*: rubbish.

wine, if thou hast no name to be known by, let us call
275 thee devil.

Iago

What was he that you followed with your sword? What
had he done to you?

Cassio

I know not.

Iago

Is't possible?

Cassio

280 I remember a mass of things, but nothing distinctly: a
quarrel, but nothing wherefore. O God, that men
should put an enemy in their mouths to steal away
their brains! That we should with joy, pleasance, revel
and applause transform ourselves into beasts!

Iago

285 Why, but you are now well enough! How came you
thus recovered?

Cassio

It hath pleased the devil drunkenness to give place to
the devil wrath: one unperfectness shows me another,
to make me frankly despise myself.

Iago

290 Come, you are too severe a moraller. As the time, the
place and the condition of this country stands, I could
heartily wish this had not so befallen: but since it is as
it is, mend it for your own good.

Cassio

I will ask him for my place again; he shall tell me I am a
295 drunkard. Had I as many mouths as Hydra, such an
answer would stop them all. To be now a sensible man,
by and by a fool, and presently a beast! O strange!
Every inordinate cup is unblessed and the ingredience
is a devil.

Iago

300 Come, come; good wine is a good familiar creature if it
be well used: exclaim no more against it. And, good
lieutenant, I think you think I love you.

Cassio

I have well approved it, sir. I drunk!

Iago

You or any man living may be drunk at a time, man.
305 I'll tell you what you shall do. Our general's wife is
now the general. I may say so in this respect, for that he

281 *nothing wherefore*: not what it was about.

283 *pleasance*: pleasure.
284 *applause*: i.e. the desire for applause.

288 *unperfectness*: imperfection.
289 *frankly*: completely.

290 *moraller*: moralist.
292 *heartily*: with all my heart.
   so befallen: happened like this.
295 *Hydra*: In classical mythology, this was a
   snake with many heads; it was killed by
   Hercules.
296 *stop*: silence.
   now: at one moment.
   sensible: Here the word has its modern
   meaning.
297 *by and by*: very soon.
   presently: now.
298 *every inordinate cup*: every drink too
   many.
   unblessed: cursed.
   the ingredience is: it contains.
300 *familiar creature*: friendly spirit; animals
   used by witches for black magic were
   commonly called 'familiars'.
301 *exclaim ... it*: stop grumbling at it.
303 *approved it*: put it to the test.

304 *at a time*: at some time.

308 *mark*: observation.
     parts: qualities.
310 *put you ... again*: get your job back.
     free: generous.

314 *splinter*: mend (by putting on a splint).
315 *lay*: bet.
315-16 *this crack ... before*: i.e. as a mended
     bone is said to be stronger than before it
     was broken.

319 *I think it freely*: I well believe it.
     betimes: early.
320 *undertake*: take up the matter.
321 *am desperate*: despair.
     check: stop.
326 Verse returns as Iago voices his intimate
     thoughts, apparently addressing the
     audience.
328 *Probal*: Reasonable.
330 *inclining*: sympathetic.
     subdue: persuade.
331 *framed as fruitful*: naturally as generous.
332 *free elements*: the four elements out of
     which all things are created; although this
     should be praise of Desdemona's
     sympathetic generosity, Iago makes it sound
     as though he despises these qualities.
333 *win*: persuade; Iago believes that
     Desdemona has such influence over Othello
     that for her sake he would even change his
     religion.
     his baptism: i.e. his Christian faith.
334 All signs and symbols (such as the sign of
     the cross) that belong to the Christian
     religion, which believes that man's sin has
     been paid for ('redeemed') by the sacrifice
     of Jesus Christ.
335 *enfettered to*: bound by.
336 *list*: wishes.
337-8 To such an extent ('Even as') that his
     desire for her ('her appetite') is like a god
     controlling his reason ('function').
339 *parallel*: i.e. to Iago's plot.
340 *Divinity*: Theology.
341 *put on*: encourage.
342 *suggest*: tempt.

hath devoted and given up himself to the contemplation, mark, and denotement of her parts and graces. Confess yourself freely to her; importune her

310 help to put you in your place again. She is of so free, so kind, so apt, so blessed a disposition, that she holds it a vice in her goodness not to do more than she is requested. This broken joint between you and her husband, entreat her to splinter; and my fortunes

315 against any lay worth naming, this crack of your love shall grow stronger than it was before.

Cassio
You advise me well.

Iago
I protest in the sincerity of love and honest kindness.

Cassio
I think it freely; and betimes in the morning I will

320 beseech the virtuous Desdemona to undertake for me. I am desperate of my fortunes if they check me here.

Iago
You are in the right. Good night, lieutenant, I must to the watch.

Cassio
325 Good night, honest Iago.   [*Exit*

Iago
And what's he then that says I play the villain,
When this advice is free I give, and honest,
Probal to thinking, and indeed the course
To win the Moor again? For 'tis most easy

330 Th'inclining Desdemona to subdue
In any honest suit. She's framed as fruitful
As the free elements; and then for her
To win the Moor—were't to renounce his baptism,
All seals and symbols of redeemèd sin—

335 His soul is so enfettered to her love,
That she may make, unmake, do what she list,
Even as her appetite shall play the god
With his weak function. How am I then a villain
To counsel Cassio to this parallel course

340 Directly to his good? Divinity of hell!
When devils will the blackest sins put on,
They do suggest at first with heavenly shows
As I do now. For whiles this honest fool

344 *Plies*: Pleads with.

347 *repeals*: wants to have him reinstated.
348-9 By however much effort she tries to help Cassio, she will lose favour ('undo her credit') with Othello.
350 *virtue into pitch*: virtue is usually depicted as white, whereas *pitch* is a sticky, foul-smelling, black substance.

353 *chase*: hunt.
354 *fills up the cry*: makes up the number of the pack and adds its voice to the sound of the hunt; Roderigo has, unwittingly, adopted the imagery used by Iago at the end of *Act 2, Scene 2*.
356 *cudgelled*: beaten.
358 *wit*: sense.
361 *wit*: cunning.
362 *dilatory*: dawdling.
364 *cashiered Cassio*: got Cassio dismissed (Iago seems to enjoy the alliteration of these words).
365-6 Another one of Iago's cryptic remarks: most things grow well in the sunshine, but the fruits that are the first to blossom are also the earliest to ripen. Cassio's dismissal is the first sign of success—the 'blossom'—for Roderigo.
367 *'tis morning*: The time has passed quickly; it was not ten o'clock at night when the scene started (line 13).
369 *Retire thee*: Get out of the way.
 where thou art billeted: to your lodgings.
370 *hereafter*: later.

372 *move*: plead.
373 *set her on*: urge her.
374 *the while*: meanwhile.
 apart: aside.
375 *jump*: at the precise moment.
376 *Soliciting*: Asking favours.
377 *device*: scheme.

Plies Desdemona to repair his fortunes
345 And she for him pleads strongly to the Moor,
I'll pour this pestilence into his ear:
That she repeals him for her body's lust!
And by how much she strives to do him good,
She shall undo her credit with the Moor.
350 So will I turn her virtue into pitch,
And out of her own goodness make the net
That shall enmesh them all.

Enter Roderigo

How now, Roderigo?
Roderigo
I do follow here in the chase, not like a hound that hunts, but one that fills up the cry. My money is
355 almost spent; I have been tonight exceedingly well cudgelled; and I think the issue will be, I shall have so much experience for my pains; and so, with no money at all, and a little more wit, return again to Venice.
Iago
How poor are they that have not patience!
360 What wound did ever heal but by degrees?
Thou know'st we work by wit, and not by witchcraft,
And wit depends on dilatory time.
Does't not go well? Cassio hath beaten thee,
And thou by that small hurt hath cashiered Cassio.
365 Though other things grow fair against the sun,
Yet fruits that blossom first will first be ripe.
Content thyself awhile. By th'mass, 'tis morning:
Pleasure and action make the hours seem short.
Retire thee; go where thou art billeted.
370 Away, I say; thou shalt know more hereafter:
Nay, get thee gone.   [*Exit* Roderigo
            Two things are to be done.
My wife must move for Cassio to her mistress:
I'll set her on.
Myself the while to draw the Moor apart,
375 And bring him jump when he may Cassio find
Soliciting his wife. Ay, that's the way.
Dull not device by coldness and delay.   [*Exit*

Act 3

Act 3   Scene 1

Musicians, hired by Cassio, are playing outside Othello's lodgings in Cyprus; but the Clown sends them away. Cassio asks to see Emilia, and when she appears he begs for her help in gaining access to Desdemona. The music, and the Clown's feeble jokes, give a momentary relief from the tension built up in the previous scene.

1 *content your pains*: pay you for your trouble.
2 *bid ... general*: It was a courtly Elizabethan custom to wake the newly-married couple with a song.
4 *in Naples ... nose*: The Neapolitan accent may have been rather nasal in sound; *and* the Clown is attempting some poor sexual joke based on the 'Neapolitan disease', which was a venereal condition.
5 What do you mean?
6 *wind instruments*: probably a form of bagpipe (see line 19).

7 Yes, indeed.
8 There's a story ('tale') to be told there; but the Clown is also making a pun on 'tail' = penis.
15 *to't again*: play some more.

Scene 1

Enter Cassio *and* Musicians

Cassio
Masters, play here—I will content your pains—
Something that's brief; and bid 'Good morrow, general'.

                                          [*They play*
Enter Clown

Clown
Why, masters, have your instruments been in Naples, that they speak i'th'nose thus?

First Musician
5 How, sir, how?

Clown
Are these, I pray you, wind instruments?

First Musician
Ay, marry are they, sir.

Clown
O, thereby hangs a tail.

First Musician
Whereby hangs a tale, sir?

Clown
10 Marry, sir, by many a wind instrument that I know. But, masters, here's money for you: and the general so likes your music that he desires you, for love's sake, to make no more noise with it.

First Musician
Well, sir, we will not.

Clown
15 If you have any music that may not be heard, to't again. But, as they say, to hear music the general does not greatly care.

First Musician
We have none such, sir.

Clown
Then put up your pipes in your bag, for I'll away.
20 Go, vanish into air, away.   [*Exeunt* Musicians

Cassio
Dost thou hear, mine honest friend?

Clown
No, I hear not your honest friend: I hear you.

Cassio
Prithee keep up thy quillets—there's a poor piece
of gold for thee. If the gentlewoman that attends the
25 general's wife be stirring, tell her there's one Cassio
entreats her a little favour of speech. Wilt thou do this?

Clown
She is stirring, sir. If she will stir hither, I shall seem
to notify unto her.

Cassio
Do, good my friend.   [*Exit* Clown

Enter Iago

In happy time, Iago.

Iago
30 You have not been abed then?

Cassio
Why, no: the day had broke before we parted.
I have made bold, Iago,
To send in to your wife. My suit to her
Is that she will to virtuous Desdemona
35 Procure me some access.

Iago   I'll send her to you presently;
And I'll devise a mean to draw the Moor
Out of the way, that your converse and business
May be more free.

Cassio   I humbly thank you for't.

Exit Iago

I never knew a Florentine more kind and honest.

Enter Emilia

Emilia
40 Good morrow, good lieutenant; I am sorry
For your displeasure: but all will sure be well.
The general and his wife are talking of it,

23 *quillets*: quibbles.

25 *stirring*: awake; but the Clown makes a pun in line 27.
26 *a little favour of speech*: the favour of a few words with her.
27 *stirring*: sexually active.
28 *seem ... her*: The Clown is making fun of Cassio's courtly manners.

29 *In happy time*: You have come at the right time.
30 *abed*: to bed.

33 *suit*: request.

35 *presently*: immediately.
36 *a mean*: a way.

39 *a Florentine*: i.e. one of Cassio's own countrymen; Iago is a Venetian.

41 *your displeasure*: that you have incurred Othello's displeasure.

43 *stoutly*: loyally.
44 *of great fame*: well known.
45 *great affinity*: with important connections.
   wholesome wisdom: all commonsense.
46 *He ... you*: He could not do anything
   except dismiss you.

48 To take the first possible opportunity; the
   early emblems of Opportunity depict a
   figure who is bald behind and must be
   seized by the forelock ('by the front').
49 *in again*: back in favour.

54 *bosom*: heart.
   much bound: very grateful.

And she speaks for you stoutly. The Moor replies
That he you hurt is of great fame in Cyprus,
45 And great affinity; and that in wholesome wisdom
He might not but refuse you; but he protests he
   loves you
And needs no other suitor but his likings
To take the safest occasion by the front
To bring you in again.
    Cassio   Yet I beseech you,
50 If you think fit, or that it may be done,
Give me advantage of some brief discourse
With Desdemona alone.
    Emilia   Pray you, come in:
I will bestow you where you shall have time
To speak your bosom freely.
    Cassio   I am much bound to you.
                       [*Exeunt*

Act 3   Scene 2

Othello leaves home for the morning—and
the audience knows that Desdemona will be
alone.

1 *letters ... pilot*: Othello is sending letters to
  Venice which the pilot of the ship will
  carry.
2 *do my duties*: pay my respects.
3 *works*: fortifications.
4 *Repair*: Return.

Scene 2

    Enter Othello, Iago, *and* Gentlemen

    Othello
These letters give, Iago, to the pilot,
And by him do my duties to the senate.
That done, I will be walking on the works:
Repair there to me.
    Iago   Well, my good lord, I'll do't.   [*Exit*
    Othello
5 This fortification, gentlemen, shall we see't?
    Gentlemen
We'll wait upon your lordship.   [*Exeunt*

Act 3   Scene 3

Cassio, having obtained Desdemona's
promise of help, takes his leave—but not
before Othello has seen him with
Desdemona. Iago is quick to rouse Othello's
suspicions, and when Desdemona begins to
plead for Cassio she finds little response

Scene 3

    Enter Desdemona, Cassio, *and* Emilia

    Desdemona
Be thou assured, good Cassio, I will do
All my abilities in thy behalf.

from her husband. Iago renews his attack on the Moor, whose trust in Desdemona begins to waver. When Desdemona drops her handkerchief it is picked up by Emilia, who gives it to her husband. Othello returns and Iago continues to stimulate his jealous suspicions. The Moor is at last convinced. His trust in Desdemona is shattered, and he vows revenge. Iago promises assistance. In this, the central scene of the play, Othello begins to lose control of the situation and Iago takes possession.

12 *strangeness*: unfriendliness.
13 *politic*: politically necessary.
14-16 The precise sense of these lines is unclear. Cassio seems to be afraid that Othello's policy (of making Cassio's dismissal an example of good discipline) may continue for too long, or be prolonged for such poor reasons, or even be continued without any reason.
15 *nice*: thin.
16 *circumstance*: reason.
17 *supplied*: taken by someone else.

19 *doubt*: fear.
    Before: In presence of.
20 *warrant*: promise.
21 *friendship*: friendly action.
22 *last article*: very end.
23 *watch him*: keep him awake (hawks were tamed by being kept awake).
    talk ... patience: talk to him until he can endure it no longer.
24 *board*: table.
    shrift: confessional—where the penitent is given instruction after his confession.
25 *intermingle*: mix.
27 *solicitor*: the one who pleads for him—i.e. herself.
28 *give ... away*: give up your case.

33 *purposes*: good.

Emilia
Good madam, do: I warrant it grieves my husband
As if the case were his.
Desdemona
5 O that's an honest fellow! Do not doubt, Cassio,
But I will have my lord and you again
As friendly as you were.
Cassio   Bounteous madam,
Whatever shall become of Michael Cassio,
He's never anything but your true servant.
Desdemona
10 I know't: I thank you. You do love my lord;
You have known him long, and be you well assured
He shall in strangeness stand no farther off
Than in a politic distance.
Cassio   Ay, but, lady,
That policy may either last so long,
15 Or feed upon such nice and waterish diet,
Or breed itself so out of circumstance,
That I being absent and my place supplied,
My general will forget my love and service.
Desdemona
Do not doubt that. Before Emilia here,
20 I give thee warrant of thy place. Assure thee,
If I do vow a friendship, I'll perform it
To the last article. My lord shall never rest.
I'll watch him tame and talk him out of patience;
His bed shall seem a school, his board a shrift;
25 I'll intermingle everything he does
With Cassio's suit. Therefore be merry, Cassio,
For thy solicitor shall rather die
Than give thy cause away.

Enter Othello *and* Iago

Emilia
Madam, here comes my lord.
Cassio
30 Madam, I'll take my leave.
Desdemona
Why stay, and hear me speak.
Cassio
Madam, not now: I am very ill at ease,
Unfit for mine own purposes.

34 *your discretion*: as you think best.

35 *I like not that*: Iago begins his campaign.

47 Make peace with him at once.

49 *in cunning*: deliberately.

55 *Desdemon*: Shakespeare abbreviates Desdemona's name, partly to let Othello speak affectionately—and partly for the rhythm of the line.

58 *dinner*: the meal eaten at mid-day.

Desdemona
Well, do your discretion.   [*Exit* Cassio

Iago
35 Ha! I like not that.
      Othello   What dost thou say?
Iago
Nothing, my lord; or if—I know not what.
Othello
Was not that Cassio parted from my wife?
Iago
Cassio, my lord? No, sure, I cannot think it
That he would sneak away so guilty-like,
40 Seeing you coming.
      Othello   I do believe 'twas he.
Desdemona
How now, my lord?
I have been talking with a suitor here,
A man that languishes in your displeasure.
Othello
Who is't you mean?
Desdemona
45 Why, your lieutenant, Cassio. Good my lord,
If I have any grace or power to move you,
His present reconciliation take.
For if he be not one that truly loves you,
That errs in ignorance, and not in cunning,
50 I have no judgement in an honest face.
I prithee call him back.
      Othello   Went he hence now?
Desdemona
Yes, faith; so humbled
That he hath left part of his grief with me
To suffer with him. Good love, call him back.
Othello
55 Not now, sweet Desdemon; some other time.
Desdemona
But shall't be shortly?
      Othello   The sooner, sweet, for you.
Desdemona
Shall't be tonight, at supper?
      Othello   No, not tonight.
Desdemona
Tomorrow dinner then?
      Othello   I shall not dine at home.

I meet the captains at the citadel.

Desdemona

60 Why, then, tomorrow night, or Tuesday morn,
On Tuesday noon, or night; on Wednesday morn.
I prithee name the time, but let it not
Exceed three days. In faith, he's penitent:
And yet his trespass, in our common reason—
65 Save that, they say, the wars must make example
Out of their best—is not almost a fault
T'incur a private check. When shall he come?
Tell me, Othello. I wonder in my soul
What you would ask me that I should deny,
70 Or stand so mammering on? What! Michael Cassio,
That came a-wooing with you? And so many a
   time—
When I have spoke of you dispraisingly—
Hath ta'en your part, to have so much to do
To bring him in? By'r Lady, I could do much.

Othello

75 Prithee, no more: let him come when he will;
I will deny thee nothing.

Desdemona   Why, this is not a boon:
'Tis as I should entreat you wear your gloves
Or feed on nourishing dishes, or keep you warm,
Or sue to you to do a peculiar profit
80 To your own person. Nay, when I have a suit
Wherein I mean to touch your love indeed
It shall be full of poise and difficult weight,
And fearful to be granted.

Othello   I will deny thee nothing.
Whereon, I do beseech thee, grant me this:
85 To leave me but a little to my self.

Desdemona

Shall I deny you? No; farewell, my lord.

Othello

Farewell, my Desdemona, I'll come to thee straight.

Desdemona

Emilia, come. Be as your fancies teach you.
Whate'er you be, I am obedient.

          Exeunt Desdemona *and* Emilia

Othello

90 Excellent wretch! Perdition catch my soul
But I do love thee! And when I love thee not,
Chaos is come again.

---

64 *in ... reason*: by normal standards.
65-6 *example ... best*: even the highest officers must be made an example to the other soldiers; see 2,3,244.
66-7 *is not ... check*: is hardly worth a private rebuke (not to mention Cassio's public disgrace).

70 *mammering on*: hesitating.

74 *bring him in*: i.e. back in favour.
    By'r Lady: Desdemona swears by the Virgin Mary.
75 *will*: wishes.

76 *boon*: personal favour (for herself).
77 *as*: as if.

79 *peculiar*: personal.
    profit: benefit.
81 *touch ... indeed*: really put your love to the test.
82 *poise ... weight*: the metaphor is from scales, where weights are balanced (poised) in different pans.
83 *fearful*: a serious matter.
84 *Whereon*: At this point.

87 *straight*: immediately.

88 *fancies*: desires.
90 *wretch*: the term is used affectionately.
    Perdition catch my soul: Damn me.
91 *But I do love thee*: If I do not love you.
92 *Chaos is come again*: i.e. It will be the end of the world; the Elizabethans believed that at the end of the world all things would return to the state of chaos that existed before creation.

Iago   My noble lord—

Othello

What dost thou say, Iago?

Iago   Did Michael Cassio,

When you wooed my lady, know of your love?

Othello

95 He did, from first to last. Why dost thou ask?

Iago

But for a satisfaction of my thought—

No further harm.

Othello   Why of thy thought, Iago?

Iago

I did not think he had been acquainted with her.

Othello

O yes, and went between us very oft.

Iago

100 Indeed?

Othello

Indeed? Ay, indeed. Discern'st thou aught in that?

Is he not honest?

Iago   Honest, my lord?

Othello   Honest? Ay, honest.

Iago

My lord, for aught I know.

Othello   What dost thou think?

Iago

Think, my lord?

Othello

105 Think, my lord! By heaven, he echoes me,

As if there were some monster in his thought

Too hideous to be shown. Thou dost mean

    something.

I heard thee say even now, thou lik'st not that,

When Cassio left my wife. What did'st not like?

110 And when I told thee he was of my counsel

In my whole course of wooing, thou cried'st

    'Indeed!'

And didst contract and purse thy brow together,

As if thou then hadst shut up in thy brain

Some horrible conceit. If thou dost love me,

115 Show me thy thought.

Iago

My lord, you know I love you.

96 *But ... thought*: I just wondered.

99 *went between us*: i.e. carrying messages.

100 *Indeed*: The actor playing Iago is directed how to react by Othello's description of his behaviour at line 112.
101 *Discern'st ... that*: Can you see anything wrong in that; Iago is beginning to irritate Othello.
102 *honest*: trustworthy; but the word has many meanings in this play.

110 *of my counsel*: in my confidence.
111 *course of wooing*: courtship.

112 *contract ... brow*: frown.
113 *shut up in thy brain*: you were thinking in your head.
114 *conceit*: idea.
115 *Show*: Tell.

118 *weigh'st*: consider.
    giv'st them breath: speak them.
119 *stops*: hesitations.
121 *tricks of custom*: usual.
    just: trustworthy.
122-3 *close dilations*: secret utterances which
    are heartfelt ('working from the heart') and
    which cannot be controlled ('passion cannot
    rule').

126 *be not*: i.e. are not what they seem.
    would ... none: I wish they would not
    seem what they are not.
130 *speak ... thinkings*: tell me what you really
    think.
131 *As thou dost ruminate*: When you really
    think it over.
134 *to that ... free to*: to that which all slaves
    are free to do—i.e. think their own
    thoughts.
135 *they*: i.e his thoughts.
136 *As where's*: Where, for example.
137-140 *Who ... lawful*: In an extended
    metaphor Iago asks whether anyone's mind
    can be so pure that unclean thoughts do not
    enter into it in company with decent ideas.
138 *apprehensions*: ideas.
139 *leets*: local courts.
    law-days: the days on which courts of law
    are held.
    in session sit: sit like judges in a law-
    court.
140 *meditations lawful*: respectable thoughts.
141 *conspire*: plot.
    against thy friend: i.e. against Othello
    himself.
142-3 *mak'st ... thoughts*: don't tell him what
    you are thinking.
144 *perchance*: perhaps.
    vicious in my guess: badly misinterpret;
    Iago's present speech is uncharacteristic,
    lacking the directness of his usual
    utterances—and its very indirectness makes
    Othello wary.
145 *my nature's plague*: I can't help this bad
    habit.
146 *jealousy*: suspicion.
147 *Shapes*: Imagines.

Othello   I think thou dost:
And for I know thou'rt full of love and honesty,
And weigh'st thy words before thou giv'st them
    breath,
Therefore these stops of thine affright me more:
120 For such things in a false disloyal knave
Are tricks of custom; but in a man that's just,
They're close dilations, working from the heart,
That passion cannot rule.
    Iago   For Michael Cassio,
I dare be sworn I think that he is honest.
    Othello
125 I think so too.
    Iago   Men should be what they seem;
Or those that be not, would they might seem none!
    Othello
Certain, men should be what they seem.
    Iago
Why, then, I think Cassio's an honest man.
    Othello
Nay, yet there's more in this.
130 I prithee speak to me as to thy thinkings,
As thou dost ruminate, and give thy worst of
    thoughts
The worst of words.
    Iago   Good my lord, pardon me;
Though I am bound to every act of duty,
I am not bound to that all slaves are free to:
135 Utter my thoughts. Why, say they are vile and false?
As where's that palace whereinto foul things
Sometimes intrude not? Who has a breast so pure,
But some uncleanly apprehensions
Keep leets and law-days, and in session sit
140 With meditations lawful?
    Othello
Thou dost conspire against thy friend, Iago,
If thou but think'st him wronged, and mak'st his ear
A stranger to thy thoughts.
    Iago   I do beseech you,
Though I perchance am vicious in my guess—
145 As I confess it is my nature's plague
To spy into abuses, and oft my jealousy
Shapes faults that are not—that your wisdom then,

148 *conceits*: understands.

150 *scattering*: casual.
     observance: observation.
151 *quiet*: peace of mind.

155 *immediate*: most precious, nearest the
     heart.

158 *filches*: steals.

161-2 Even if Othello were to kill Iago, he
       would not be able to find his thoughts; and
       as long as Iago is alive, he will not disclose
       them.
162 *'tis ... custody*: it (i.e. his heart) is in
     Iago's keeping.

163 *jealousy*: suspicion of sexual infidelity.
164 *green-eyed monster*: green is traditionally
     the colour of jealousy.
164-5 *mock ... on*: the more jealous a man is,
       the more ridiculous he becomes.
165 *That*: Any.
     cuckold: man cheated (sexually) by his
     wife.
166 *certain of his fate*: sure that his wife has
     been false.
     wronger: the wife who has deceived him.
167 *tells*: counts.
171 *fineless*: infinite.
172 *ever*: always.
176-7 *To follow ... suspicions*: To experience
       new doubts several times a month, as the
       moon waxes and wanes.

177-8 *To be ... resolved*: As soon as I have any
       doubt, I will settle the question.
178 *a goat*: a creature reputedly lustful.
179 *turn ... soul*: give my mind to thinking.

From one that so imperfectly conceits,
Would take no notice, nor build yourself a trouble
150 Out of his scattering and unsure observance.
It were not for your quiet nor your good,
Nor for my manhood, honesty, and wisdom,
To let you know my thoughts.
     Othello   What dost thou mean?
     Iago
Good name in man and woman, dear my lord,
155 Is the immediate jewel of their souls.
Who steals my purse, steals trash; 'tis something,
    nothing;
'Twas mine, 'tis his, and has been slave to
    thousands:
But he that filches from me my good name
Robs me of that which not enriches him
160 And makes me poor indeed.
     Othello   By heaven, I'll know thy thoughts.
     Iago
You cannot, if my heart were in your hand,
Nor shall not, whilst 'tis in my custody.
     Othello
Ha!
     Iago   O beware, my lord, of jealousy!
It is the green-eyed monster, which doth mock
165 The meat it feeds on. That cuckold lives in bliss
Who, certain of his fate, loves not his wronger;
But O, what damnèd minutes tells he o'er,
Who dotes yet doubts, suspects yet fondly loves!
     Othello
O misery!
     Iago
170 Poor and content is rich, and rich enough;
But riches fineless is as poor as winter,
To him that ever fears he shall be poor.
Good God, the souls of all my tribe defend
From jealousy!
     Othello   Why, why is this?
175 Think'st thou I'd make a life of jealousy,
To follow still the changes of the moon
With fresh suspicions? No, to be once in doubt
Is once to be resolved. Exchange me for a goat,
When I shall turn the business of my soul

180 *exsufflicate*: blown up, exaggerated; the context seems to demand such a meaning—there is no other known use of the word.
    blown: fly-blown, rotten.
    surmises: suspicions.
181 *Matching thy inference*: To equal your interpretation.
    'Tis not: It does not.
185 *mine own weak merits*: the fact that I do not deserve to have her.
186 *revolt*: infidelity.
187 *had eyes*: knew what I was like.
188 *I'll see*: I want evidence.

193 *bound*: in duty bound to speak.
194 *Receive ... me*: Let me tell you.
195 *Look to*: Take care of.

196 *secure*: over-confident.

198 *self-bounty*: its own goodness.
199 *our country disposition*: how the people [i.e. the women] of my nation behave.
200 *pranks*: sexual tricks.
201 *best conscience*: highest moral standard.

205-6 Desdemona deceived Othello by pretending to be frightened of him when in fact she loved him most.
206 *Why, go to, then*: Then that proves it (i.e. that Desdemona is deceptive).
207 *Seeming*: pretence.
208 *seel*: close up, blind.
    close as oak: oak is a very strong, close-grained wood, and a door made of oak is hard to open.
209 *He ... witchcraft*: Brabantio thought that witchcraft was responsible for Desdemona's conduct.
210-11 Please forgive me for loving you too much.
211 *bound*: indebted.

180 To such exsufflicate and blown surmises,
Matching thy inference. 'Tis not to make me jealous
To say my wife is fair, loves company,
Is free of speech, sings, plays, and dances well:
Where virtue is, these are more virtuous.
185 Nor from mine own weak merits will I draw
The smallest fear or doubt of her revolt,
For she had eyes and chose me. No, Iago,
I'll see before I doubt; when I doubt, prove;
And on the proof, there is no more but this:
190 Away at once with love or jealousy!

Iago
I am glad of this: for now I shall have reason
To show the love and duty that I bear you
With franker spirit. Therefore, as I am bound,
Receive it from me. I speak not yet of proof.
195 Look to your wife; observe her well with Cassio.
Wear your eye thus: not jealous, nor secure.
I would not have your free and noble nature,
Out of self-bounty, be abused. Look to't.
I know our country disposition well:
200 In Venice they do let God see the pranks
They dare not show their husbands; their best conscience
Is not to leave't undone, but keep't unknown.

Othello
Dost thou say so?

Iago
She did deceive her father, marrying you,
205 And when she seemed to shake, and fear your looks,
She loved them most.

Othello   And so she did.

Iago   Why, go to, then!
She that so young could give out such a seeming,
To seel her father's eyes up close as oak—
He thought 'twas witchcraft. —But I am much to blame,
210 I humbly do beseech you of your pardon
For too much loving you.

Othello   I am bound to thee for ever.

Iago
I see this hath a little dashed your spirits.

213 *Not a jot*: Not at all.

Othello

Not a jot, not a jot.

Iago   In faith, I fear it has.

I hope you will consider what is spoke

215 *moved*: distressed.
216 *I am to pray you*: I must beg you.
    strain: force.
217 *issues*: conclusions.
217–18 *nor to ... suspicion*: extend beyond
    suspicion.

215 Comes from my love. But I do see you're moved.

I am to pray you, not to strain my speech

To grosser issues, nor to larger reach

Than to suspicion.

Othello

I will not.

Iago   Should you do so, my lord,

220 *fall ... success*: have such a dreadful result.
221 *aimed not at*: did not intend.

220 My speech should fall into such vile success

Which my thoughts aimed not at. Cassio's my

    worthy friend.

My lord, I see you're moved.

Othello   No, not much moved.

223 *honest*: chaste.

I do not think but Desdemona's honest.

Iago

Long live she so! And long live you to think so!

Othello

225 *erring from itself*: straying from its true
self.

225 And yet, how nature erring from itself—

Iago

226 *to be bold with you*: to put it to you
bluntly.
227 *affect*: like.
228 *clime*: country.

Ay, there's the point: as, to be bold with you,

Not to affect many proposèd matches

Of her own clime, complexion, and degree,

Whereto we see in all things nature tends—

231 *disproportion*: impropriety.
232 *in position*: positively.
233 *Distinctly*: Specifically.
234 *recoiling*: returning.
235 *fall to match*: come to compare.
    her country forms: the appearances of her
countrymen.
236 *happily*: perhaps.

230 Foh! One may smell in such a will most rank,

Foul disproportion, thoughts unnatural.

But, pardon me, I do not in position

Distinctly speak of her, though I may fear

Her will, recoiling to her better judgement,

235 May fall to match you with her country forms,

And happily repent.

Othello   Farewell, farewell.

If more thou dost perceive, let me know more.

Set on thy wife to observe. Leave me, Iago.

Iago

[*Going*] My lord, I take my leave.

Othello

240 Why did I marry? This honest creature doubtless

Sees and knows more, much more than he unfolds.

241 *unfolds*: reveals.

Iago

[*Returning*] My lord, I would I might entreat your

    honour

243 *scan*: consider.
244 *place*: position (as lieutenant).

247 *means*: methods.
248 *strain ... entertainment*: urges his reinstatement.
249 *importunity*: pleading.

251 *busy*: interfering.

253 *hold her free*: think her innocent.

254 *my government*: my self-control.

256 *qualities*: types.
     with a learnèd spirit: from experience.
257 *haggard*: a wild, untrained hawk.
258 *jesses*: the straps which secure the hawk's legs.

259 *whistle her off*: cast her off.
     let her down the wind: the hawk that was released to hunt down wind rarely returned to the hunter's fist.
260 *prey at fortune*: take her own chances, look after herself.
     Haply: Perhaps.
     for: because.
261 *soft ... conversation*: easy social manners.
262 *chamberers*: gallants, 'social types', 'ladies' men'.
262-3 *declined ... years*: older.
264 *abused*: deceived.
     relief: reaction.
267 *appetites*: desires.
     toad: traditionally a loathsome creature.
268 *vapour*: foul air; dungeons were often the sewers of a castle.
271 *Prerogatived ... base*: They have even less chance to escape cuckoldry than poor men have.

To scan this thing no farther. Leave it to time.
Although 'tis fit that Cassio have his place,
245 For sure he fills it up with great ability,
Yet, if you please to hold him off awhile,
You shall by that perceive him and his means;
Note if your lady strain his entertainment
With any strong or vehement importunity—
250 Much will be seen in that. In the meantime,
Let me be thought too busy in my fears
(As worthy cause I have to fear I am)
And hold her free, I do beseech your honour.
     Othello
Fear not my government.
     Iago   I once more take my leave.
                                        [*Exit*
     Othello
255 This fellow's of exceeding honesty,
And knows all qualities, with a learnèd spirit,
Of human dealings. If I do prove her haggard,
Though that her jesses were my dear heart-strings,
I'd whistle her off, and let her down the wind
260 To prey at fortune. Haply for I am black
And have not those soft parts of conversation
That chamberers have; or for I am declined
Into the vale of years—yet that's not much—
She's gone: I am abused, and my relief
265 Must be to loathe her. O curse of marriage,
That we can call these delicate creatures ours
And not their appetites! I had rather be a toad
And live upon the vapour of a dungeon
Than keep a corner in the thing I love
270 For others' uses. Yet 'tis the plague of great ones;
Prerogatived are they less than the base.
'Tis destiny unshunnable, like death:
Even then this forkèd plague is fated to us
When we do quicken. Desdemona comes!

     Enter Desdemona *and* Emilia

275 If she be false, O then heaven mocks itself!
I'll not believe't.
     Desdemona   How now, my dear Othello!
Your dinner, and the generous islanders
By you invited, do attend your presence.

272 *destiny unshunnable*: inescapable fate.
273–4 *Even then ... do quicken*: We are
    destined to be cuckolded from the very
    moment when we are born.
273 *forkèd plague*: the cuckolded man was said
    to grow horns (forks) on his head, which
    could be seen by all except himself.
277 *generous*: noble.
278 *attend*: await.
279 *I am to blame*: Othello may be
    apologizing for his delay in coming into
    dinner; *or* blaming himself for his suspicion
    of Desdemona.
    faintly: softly.
281 *pain upon my forehead*: i.e. where the
    cuckold's horns would grow.
282 *watching*: lack of sleep.
284 *napkin*: handkerchief.

288 *remembrance*: keepsake.
289 *wayward*: wilful.
290 *Wooed*: Persuaded.
291 *conjured her*: made her swear.
292 *reserves*: keeps.
293 *work*: embroidery.
    ta'en out: copied.
296 *I ... fantasy*: I have nothing to do with it,
    except that I'm satisfying his whim
    ('fantasy').

297 *do you*: are you doing.

299 *thing*: Iago pretends to understand the
    word in its Elizabethan slang sense (= the
    female sexual organ); he implies that Emilia
    does not keep this for him, but makes it
    'common'—i.e. available to all.

303 *that same handkerchief*: i.e. the one he
    has talked about.

Othello
I am to blame.
Desdemona   Why do you speak so faintly?
280 Are you not well?
    Othello
I have a pain upon my forehead here.
    Desdemona
Faith, that's with watching: 'twill away again.
Let me but bind it hard, within this hour
It will be well.
    Othello   Your napkin is too little.
    He puts the handkerchief from him, and
    she drops it
285 Let it alone. Come, I'll go in with you.
    Desdemona
I am very sorry that you are not well.
        [Exeunt Othello *and* Desdemona
    Emilia
I am glad I have found this napkin:
This was her first remembrance from the Moor.
My wayward husband hath a hundred times
290 Wooed me to steal it; but she so loves the token—
For he conjured her she should ever keep it—
That she reserves it evermore about her
To kiss and talk to. I'll have the work ta'en out,
And give't Iago.
295 What he will do with it, heaven knows, not I:
I nothing, but to please his fantasy.

    Enter Iago

    Iago
How now? What do you here alone?
    Emilia
Do not you chide: I have a thing for you.
    Iago
A thing for me? It is a common thing.
    Emilia
300 Ha!
    Iago
To have a foolish wife.
    Emilia
O, is that all? What will you give me now
For that same handkerchief?

Iago   What handkerchief?
Emilia
What handkerchief!
305 Why that the Moor first gave to Desdemona;
That which so often you did bid me steal.
Iago
Hast stol'n it from her?
Emilia
No, faith, she let it drop by negligence,
And to th'advantage, I, being here, took't up.
310 Look, here it is.
Iago   A good wench! Give it me.
Emilia
What will you do with't, that you have been so
      earnest
To have me filch it?
Iago [*Snatching it*] Why, what is that to you?
Emilia
If it be not for some purpose of import,
Give't me again. Poor lady, she'll run mad
315 When she shall lack it.
Iago
Be not acknown on't: I have use for it.
Go, leave me.   [*Exit* Emilia
I will in Cassio's lodging lose this napkin,
And let him find it. Trifles light as air
320 Are to the jealous confirmations strong
As proofs of holy writ. This may do something.
The Moor already changes with my poison.
Dangerous conceits are in their natures poisons,
Which at the first are scarce found to distaste,
325 But, with a little act upon the blood,
Burn like the mines of sulphur.

Enter Othello

                                    I did say so.
Look where he comes! Not poppy, nor mandragora,
Nor all the drowsy syrups of the world,
Shall ever medicine thee to that sweet sleep
330 Which thou owed'st yesterday.
Othello   Ha, ha, false to me!

309 *to th'advantage*: luckily.

313 *import*: importance.

315 *lack it*: miss it.

316 *Be ... on't*: Say you know nothing about it.

318 *lose*: drop.

320 *confirmations*: evidence.
321 *proofs of holy writ*: words from the Bible.

323 *conceits*: imaginings.
324 *to distaste*: to be unpleasant.
325 *act*: action.
326 *mines of sulphur*: i.e. hell.

327 *poppy*: opium (derived from the poppy).
      mandragora: another narcotic plant, and its derivative.
328 *drowsy syrups*: soporific drugs.
329 *medicine*: drug.
330 *owed'st*: enjoyed.

332 *Avaunt*: Away.
     rack: an instrument of torture which stretched and twisted the limbs.
334 *but ... little*: than to have the least idea of it.
339 *wanting*: missing.
340 *Let him not know't*: As long as he doesn't know about it.
342 *the general camp*: the whole army.
343 *Pioners*: Engineers who dug trenches and were regarded as very inferior.
     tasted: enjoyed.
344 *So*: So long as.
348 *trump*: trumpet.

350 *all quality*: every attribute.
351 *circumstance*: ceremony.
352 *mortal engines*: deadly cannons.
     rude throats: loud voices.
353 *Jove's dread clamours*: i.e. thunder, caused by the thunderbolts thrown by the king of the classical gods.
354 *occupation*: i.e. his reason for living.
357 *give me the ocular proof*: let me see it with my own eyes.
360 *waked*: aroused.
362 *probation*: proof.

Iago
Why, how now, general! No more of that.

Othello
Avaunt! Be gone! Thou hast set me on the rack.
I swear 'tis better to be much abused,
Than but to know't a little.

Iago   How now, my lord!

Othello
335 What sense had I of her stolen hours of lust?
I saw't not, thought it not, it harmed not me.
I slept the next night well, was free and merry;
I found not Cassio's kisses on her lips.
He that is robbed, not wanting what is stolen,
340 Let him not know't, and he's not robbed at all.

Iago
I am sorry to hear this.

Othello
I had been happy if the general camp,
Pioners and all, had tasted her sweet body,
So I had nothing known. O now, for ever
345 Farewell the tranquil mind! Farewell content!
Farewell the plumèd troops and the big wars
That make ambition virtue—O, farewell!
Farewell the neighing steed, and the shrill trump,
The spirit-stirring drum, th'ear-piercing fife,
350 The royal banner and all quality,
Pride, pomp and circumstance of glorious war!
And, O you mortal engines, whose rude throats
Th'immortal Jove's dread clamours counterfeit,
Farewell! Othello's occupation's gone.

Iago
355 Is't possible, my lord?

Othello
Villain, be sure thou prove my love a whore;
Be sure of it: give me the ocular proof,
Or by the worth of mine eternal soul,
Thou hadst been better have been born a dog
360 Than answer my waked wrath!

Iago   Is't come to this?

Othello
Make me to see't: or, at the least, so prove it
That the probation bear no hinge nor loop
To hang a doubt on—or woe upon thy life!

Iago
My noble lord!

Othello
365 If thou dost slander her and torture me,
Never pray more; abandon all remorse;
On horror's head horrors accumulate;
Do deeds to make heaven weep, all earth amazed:
For nothing canst thou to damnation add
370 Greater than that.

Iago   O grace! O heaven defend me!
Are you a man? Have you a soul? Or sense?
God bu'y you: take mine office. O wretched fool,
That lov'st to make thine honesty a vice!
O monstrous world! Take note, take note, O world!
375 To be direct and honest is not safe.
I thank you for this profit, and from hence
I'll love no friend, sith love breeds such offence.

Othello
Nay, stay: thou shouldst be honest.

Iago
I should be wise; for honesty's a fool
380 And loses that it works for.

Othello   By the world,
I think my wife be honest, and think she is not;
I think that thou art just, and think thou art not.
I'll have some proof. Her name that was as fresh
As Dian's visage is now begrimed and black
385 As mine own face. If there be cords or knives,
Poison or fire or suffocating streams,
I'll not endure it. Would I were satisfied!

Iago
I see, sir, you are eaten up with passion.
I do repent me that I put it to you.
390 You would be satisfied?

Othello   Would! Nay, I will.

Iago
And may. But how? How satisfied, my lord?
Would you, the supervisor, grossly gape on?
Behold her topped?

Othello   Death and damnation! O!

Iago
It were a tedious difficulty, I think,
395 To bring them to that prospect. Damn them then

370 *O grace*: Iago implores the strength of divine grace to help him endure Othello's accusation.
372 *God bu'y you*: God be with you.
   take mine office: take away my appointment (as Othello's ensign or 'ancient').
   fool: Iago addresses himself.
373 *vice*: fault.
375 *direct*: outspoken.
376 *profit*: lesson I have learned.
377 *sith*: since.
   breeds such offence: causes such distress.

380 *that it works for*: the love which it tries to earn.
381 *honest*: chaste.
382 *just*: truthful.

384 *Dian*: Diana was a beautiful virgin goddess of classical mythology.
   begrimed: dirtied.
385 *cords*: ropes.
386 *suffocating streams*: water for drowning.
387 *Would I were satisfied*: I wish I were certain.
389 *put it*: suggested it.
390 *would*: want to be.

391 *How satisfied*: What would make you certain.
392 *the supervisor*: as an eye-witness.
   grossly: crudely.
393 *topped*: with a man on top of her.

395 *prospect*: situation.

396 *bolster*: share a pillow.

400 *prime*: lecherous.
    hot: lustful.
401 *salt ... in pride*: keen as wolves on heat.
401-2 *fools ... drunk*: such stupid fools as
    drunken ignorance.
403 *imputation ... circumstance*: strong
    circumstantial evidence.
404 *to the door of truth*: in the direction of
    truth.
406 *living*: valid.

407 *office*: task.
408 *sith ... far*: now that I have come so far
    with this business.
409 *Pricked*: Spurred.
410 *lay*: shared a bed.
411 *raging*: aching.

413 *loose*: indiscreet.

417 *wary*: careful.
418 *gripe*: grasp.

425 *foregone conclusion*: i.e. that a
    consummation of their love has already
    taken place.
426 *shrewd doubt*: good guess.
    though ... dream: although it was only a
    dream.
427 *thicken*: strengthen.
428 *do ... thinly*: give weaker evidence.

430 *yet*: still.

If ever mortal eyes do see them bolster
More than their own! What then? How then?
What shall I say? Where's satisfaction?
It is impossible you should see this,
400 Were they as prime as goats, as hot as monkeys,
As salt as wolves in pride, and fools as gross
As ignorance made drunk. But yet, I say,
If imputation and strong circumstance,
Which lead directly to the door of truth,
405 Will give you satisfaction, you might have't.
    Othello
Give me a living reason she's disloyal.
    Iago
I do not like the office.
But sith I am entered in this cause so far—
Pricked to't by foolish honesty and love—
410 I will go on. I lay with Cassio lately,
And being troubled with a raging tooth
I could not sleep.
There are a kind of men so loose of soul
That in their sleeps will mutter their affairs:
415 One of this kind is Cassio.
In sleep I heard him say: 'Sweet Desdemona,
Let us be wary, let us hide our loves';
And then sir, would he gripe and wring my hand,
Cry 'O sweet creature!' and then kiss me hard,
420 As if he plucked up kisses by the roots
That grew upon my lips; then laid his leg
Over my thigh, and sighed and kissed, and then
Cried 'Cursèd fate that gave thee to the Moor!'
    Othello
O monstrous! Monstrous!
    Iago   Nay, this was but his dream.
    Othello
425 But this denoted a foregone conclusion.
    Iago
'Tis a shrewd doubt, though it be but a dream:
And this may help to thicken other proofs
That do demonstrate thinly.
    Othello   I'll tear her all to pieces!
    Iago
Nay, but be wise: yet we see nothing done,
430 She may be honest yet. Tell me but this:

Have you not sometimes seen a handkerchief
Spotted with strawberries in your wife's hand?

Othello

I gave her such a one: 'twas my first gift.

Iago

I know not that: but such a handkerchief—

435   I am sure it was your wife's—did I today
See Cassio wipe his beard with.

Othello   If it be that—

Iago

If it be that, or any that was hers,
It speaks against her with the other proofs.

Othello

O, that the slave had forty thousand lives!

440   One is too poor, too weak for my revenge.
Now do I see 'tis true. Look here, Iago—
All my fond love thus do I blow to heaven:
'Tis gone.
Arise, black vengeance, from the hollow hell!

445   Yield up, O love, thy crown and hearted throne
To tyrannous hate! Swell, bosom, with thy fraught,
For 'tis of aspics' tongues!

Iago   Yet be content.

Othello

O, blood, blood, blood!

Iago

Patience, I say: your mind perhaps may change.

Othello

450   Never, Iago. Like to the Pontic sea,
Whose icy current and compulsive course
Ne'er feels retiring ebb, but keeps due on
To the Propontic and the Hellespont,
Even so my bloody thoughts, with violent pace,

455   Shall ne'er look back, ne'er ebb to humble love,
Till that a capable and wide revenge
Swallow them up. Now, by yond marble heaven,
In the due reverence of a sacred vow
I here engage my words.

He kneels

Iago   Do not rise yet.

He kneels

437   *any*: i.e. any handkerchief.
438   *speaks*: witnesses.

439   *the slave*: Othello refers to Cassio.

444   *the hollow hell*: the depths of hell.
445   *hearted throne*: throne in my heart.
446   *fraught*: burden.
447   *aspics*: poisonous snakes, whose sting would cause swelling.
         be content: calm down.

450   *Pontic sea*: the Black Sea.
451   *compulsive course*: irresistable force.
452   *Ne'er ... ebb*: Never ebbs back.
453   *the Propontic*: the Sea of Marmora.
         the Hellespont: the Dardanelles.

456   *capable and wide*: suitably great.
457   *marble*: steadfast.
458   Othello swears his revenge with the solemnity of a religious promise.
459   *engage*: pledge.

460 *ever-burning lights*: i.e. the stars.
461 *elements ... about*: the elements of fire, air, and water that enfold ('clip') the earth in the early cosmology.
463 *execution*: activity.
   wit: intellect.
465 *remorse*: compassion (because he is doing it for 'the wronged Othello' whom he refers to in line 464).
466 *What ... ever*: However murderous the job he is asked to do.

   greet: welcome.
467 *vain*: empty.
   acceptance bounteous: generous reward.

468 *upon the instant*: immediately.
   put thee to't: put you to the test.

473 *apart*: aside.
474 *furnish me*: equip myself.
475 *Now ... lieutenant*: Iago has achieved the military position he desired.

460 Witness you ever-burning lights above,
You elements, that clip us round about,
Witness that here Iago doth give up
The execution of his wit, hands, heart,
To wronged Othello's service. Let him command,
465 And to obey shall be in me remorse,
What bloody business ever.

They rise

Othello   I greet thy love,
Not with vain thanks, but with acceptance bounteous;
And will upon the instant put thee to't.
Within these three days let me hear thee say
470 That Cassio's not alive.
        Iago   My friend is dead;
'Tis done at your request. But let her live.
        Othello
Damn her, lewd minx! O, damn her, damn her!
Come go with me apart. I will withdraw
To furnish me with some swift means of death
475 For the fair devil. Now art thou my lieutenant.
        Iago
I am your own for ever.   [*Exeunt*

Act 3   Scene 4

The last scene, which charted the development of Othello's jealousy, became terrifyingly intense. Now a few weak jokes from the Clown attempt to relax the atmosphere before the action resumes.
   Desdemona has noticed that her handkerchief is lost, but she persists in her efforts to bring Cassio back into Othello's favour. Othello, however, demands the handkerchief, insisting on its magical powers. Desdemona is distressed, and Emilia is amazed. Othello leaves the stage, giving opportunity for Iago to bring Cassio to Desdemona. He pleads with her, and although Desdemona is upset, she promises to give what help she can and leaves Cassio so that she can seek out her husband. The missing handkerchief is produced when Cassio gives it to Bianca, his mistress.

Scene 4

Enter Desdemona, Emilia, *and* Clown

Desdemona
Do you know, sirrah, where lieutenant Cassio lies?
        Clown
I dare not say he lies anywhere.
        Desdemona
Why, man?
        Clown
He's a soldier, and for one to say a soldier lies is
5 stabbing.
        Desdemona
Go to! Where lodges he?
        Clown
To tell you where he lodges is to tell you where I lie.

1   *lies*: lodges: but the Clown pretends to
    understand 'lies' = speaks falsehoods.
5   *stabbing*: death (by stabbing).
7   *where I lie*: i.e. because he does not know.
9   *devise*: invent.
11 *to lie ... throat*: to tell a deliberate lie.
12 *edified*: instructed; the word is usually used
    in a religious context—and the Clown
    responds to this.

13 *catechize*: a method of Christian teaching,
    by question and answer.

16 *moved*: spoken to.

17 *compass*: scope.

22 *crusadoes*: gold coins (which were stamped
    with a cross).
    but: except that.

27 *humours*: moods.

29 *called*: reconciled.

30 *O ... dissemble*: How hard it is to deceive;
    or perhaps Othello is calling for strength in
    order to deceive.

32 *moist*: a damp, sweating palm was thought
    to indicate sexual awareness.

Desdemona
Can anything be made of this?
        Clown
I know not where he lodges, and for me to devise a
10 lodging, and say he lies here, or he lies there, were to
lie in mine own throat.
        Desdemona
Can you inquire him out? And be edified by report?
        Clown
I will catechize the world for him—that is, make
questions, and by them answer.
        Desdemona
15 Seek him; bid him come hither; tell him I have
moved my lord on his behalf, and hope all will be well.
        Clown
To do this is within the compass of man's wit, and
therefore I will attempt the doing of it.   [*Exit*
        Desdemona
Where should I lose that handkerchief, Emilia?
        Emilia
20 I know not, madam.
        Desdemona
Believe me, I had rather have lost my purse
Full of crusadoes; and, but my noble Moor
Is true of mind, and made of no such baseness
As jealous creatures are, it were enough
25 To put him to ill-thinking.
        Emilia   Is he not jealous?
        Desdemona
Who? He? I think the sun where he was born
Drew all such humours from him.
        Emilia   Look where he comes.

        Enter Othello

        Desdemona
I will not leave him now till Cassio
Be called to him. How is't with you, my lord?
        Othello
30 Well, my good lady. [*Aside*] O hardness to dissemble!
How do you, Desdemona?
        Desdemona   Well, my good lord.
        Othello
Give me your hand. This hand is moist, my lady.

Desdemona
It yet has felt no age, nor known no sorrow.
Othello
This argues fruitfulness and liberal heart.
35 Hot, hot and moist. This hand of yours requires
A sequester from liberty, fasting and prayer,
Much castigation, exercise devout;
For there's a young and sweating devil here
That commonly rebels. 'Tis a good hand,
40 A frank one.
Desdemona   You may, indeed, say so:
For 'twas that hand that gave away my heart.
Othello
A liberal hand! The hearts of old gave hands;
But our new heraldry is hands, not hearts.
Desdemona
I cannot speak of this. Come now, your promise.
Othello
45 What promise, chuck?
Desdemona
I have sent to bid Cassio come speak with you.
Othello
I have a salt and sorry rheum offends me:
Lend me thy handkerchief.
Desdemona   Here, my lord.
Othello
That which I gave you.
Desdemona   I have it not about me.
Othello
50 Not?
Desdemona No, faith my lord.
Othello   That is a fault.
That handkerchief
Did an Egyptian to my mother give:
She was a charmer and could almost read
The thoughts of people. She told her, while she kept it,
55 'Twould make her amiable and subdue my father
Entirely to her love; but if she lost it
Or made a gift of it, my father's eye
Should hold her loathèd, and his spirits should hunt
After new fancies. She, dying, gave it me,
60 And bid me, when my fate would have me wive,
To give it her. I did so; and take heed on't:

34 *liberal*: generous.

36 *sequester*: restraint.
37 *castigation*: discipline.

40 *frank*: revealing.

42–3 *The hearts ... hearts*: In the olden days
lovers ('hearts') used to give their hands (i.e.
in marriage), but nowadays they give their
hands only, not their hearts.
43 *new heraldry*: modern customs (the
reference is to the heraldic coat of arms
designed for new orders of nobility).
44 *speak of*: understand.
45 *chuck*: a term of endearment.

47 *salt and sorry rheum*: miserable running
cold.

52 *Egyptian*: These were believed to be the
ancestors of the modern gipsies.
53 *charmer*: enchantress.

55 *amiable*: beloved.

58 *spirits*: desires.
59 *fancies*: loves.
60 *when ... wive*: when it was my fortune to
marry.
61 *her*: i.e. his wife.
heed on't: care of it.

63 *perdition*: disaster.
64 *match*: equal.

Make it a darling like your precious eye.
To lose or give't away were such perdition
As nothing else could match.

Desdemona   Is't possible?
Othello

65 *web*: weaving.
66 *sibyl*: prophetess.
66-7 *that had ... compasses*: i.e. she was two hundred years old.
68 *prophetic fury*: frenzy of inspiration.
69 *hallowed*: sacred.
70 *mummy*: mummia—a preparation made from mummified dead bodies.
71 *Conserved of*: Prepared from.

65 'Tis true: there's magic in the web of it.
A sibyl, that had numbered in the world
The sun to course two hundred compasses,
In her prophetic fury sewed the work:
The worms were hallowed that did breed the silk,
70 And it was dyed in mummy, which the skilful
Conserved of maidens' hearts.

Desdemona   Indeed! Is't true?
Othello

72 *look to't well*: take good care of it.

Most veritable; therefore look to't well.

Desdemona

73 *would*: I wish.

Then would to God that I had never seen it!

Othello
Ha! Wherefore?

Desdemona

75 *startingly and rash*: abruptly and violently.

75 Why do you speak so startingly and rash?

Othello

76 *out o'th'way*: missing.

Is't lost? Is't gone? Speak: is't out o'th'way?

Desdemona
Heaven bless us!

77-9 The way these lines are divided between the two speakers makes for speed in their delivery.
77 *Say you*: What do you say?
78 *an if*: if perhaps.

Othello   Say you?
Desdemona   It is not lost.
But what an if it were?

Othello   How!
Desdemona
I say it is not lost.

Othello   Fetch't: let me see't.

Desdemona
80 Why, so I can, sir; but I will not now.

81 *to put ... suit*: make me forget what I wanted.

This is a trick to put me from my suit.
Pray you let Cassio be received again.

Othello

83 *misgives*: fears the worst.

Fetch me the handkerchief: my mind misgives.

Desdemona
Come, come:

85 *sufficient*: competent.

85 You'll never meet a more sufficient man.

Othello
The handkerchief!

88 *founded*: based.

Desdemona I pray, talk me of Cassio.
Othello
The handkerchief!
Desdemona A man that all his time
Hath founded his good fortunes on your love;
Shared dangers with you—
Othello
90 The handkerchief!
Desdemona I'faith you are to blame.
Othello
Zounds!   [*Exit*
Emilia
Is not this man jealous?
Desdemona   I ne'er saw this before.
Sure, there's some wonder in this handkerchief:
I am most unhappy in the loss of it.
Emilia
95 'Tis not a year or two shows us a man.
They are all but stomachs, and we all but food;
They eat us hungerly, and when they are full,
They belch us. Look you, Cassio and my husband.

Enter Iago *and* Cassio

Iago
There is no other way: 'tis she must do't.
100 And lo, the happiness! Go, and importune her.
Desdemona
How now, good Cassio! What's the news with you?
Cassio
Madam, my former suit. I do beseech you
That by your virtuous means I may again
Exist and be a member of his love,
105 Whom I, with all the office of my heart,
Entirely honour. I would not be delayed.
If my offence be of such mortal kind
That nor my service past, nor present sorrows,
Nor purposed merit in futurity,
110 Can ransom me into his love again,
But to know so must be my benefit:
So shall I clothe me in a forced content,
And shut myself up in some other course
To Fortune's alms.
Desdemona   Alas, thrice-gentle Cassio!

93 *wonder*: magic.
95 *'Tis ... man*: It doesn't take very long for us to know what men are like.
96 All men are merely appetites, and women are nothing but food to them.

97 *hungerly*: hungrily.

100 *the happiness*: what luck (to have found Desdemona).

104 *Exist*: Be myself.
105 *office*: loyalty.
106 *I would not be delayed*: I don't want to waste time.
107 *mortal*: deadly.
108 *nor ... nor*: neither ... nor.
109 *purposed merit*: what I intend to deserve.
      in futurity: in times to come.
110 *ransom*: buy my way back.
111 *But to know so*: Only to know this (i.e. the hopelessness of the situation).
      be my benefit: would be a help.
112 Then I shall have to be satisfied with that.
113 *shut myself up*: engage myself.
      some other course: a different career.
114 *To Fortune's alms*: To beg a living from fortune.

115	*advocation*: advocacy.
	in tune: suitable.
117	*favour*: appearance.
	humour: temper.
118	I swear before all the blessed angels.
119	*As*: That.
	all my best: to the best of my ability.
120	*within the blank*: at the centre of the target (in archery).
121	*free speech*: outspokenness.

115 My advocation is not now in tune:
My lord is not my lord; nor should I know him,
Were he in favour as in humour altered.
So help me every spirit sanctified
As I have spoken for you all my best,
120 And stood within the blank of his displeasure
For my free speech! You must awhile be patient.
What I can do, I will; and more I will,
Than for myself I dare. Let that suffice you.
        Iago
Is my lord angry?
        Emilia   He went hence but now
125 And certainly in strange unquietness.
        Iago
Can he be angry? I have seen the cannon
When it hath blown his ranks into the air,
And like the devil from his very arm
Puffed his own brother—and can he be angry?

130	*of moment*: very important.
131	*There's ... indeed*: It's serious then.

130 Something of moment then. I will go meet him.
There's matter in't indeed if he be angry.
        Desdemona
I prithee do so.   [*Exit* Iago
              Something, sure, of state,

132	*sure*: I'm sure.
133	*unhatched practice*: undisclosed plot.
134	*demonstrable*: obvious.
135	*puddled*: disturbed.
136	*wrangle with*: quarrel over.
137	*'Tis even so*: That must be it.
138-40	If our finger aches, it makes the whole of our body hurt.
141	*of them*: from them.
	observancy: attentiveness.
142	*the bridal*: the wedding-night.
	Beshrew me much: Desdemona swears a very mild oath.
143	*unhandsome warrior*: unskilled soldier; Desdemona remembers how Othello called her his 'fair warrior' when he greeted her in Cyprus (2, 1, 176).
144	*Arraigning*: Accusing.
	unkindness: unnatural behaviour.
145	*suborned the witness*: caused the witness [i.e. herself] to give false evidence.
146	*indicted*: accused.
147	*state matters*: affairs of state.
148	*conception*: fantasy.
	toy: fancy.

Either from Venice, or some unhatched practice
Made demonstrable here in Cyprus to him,
135 Hath puddled his clear spirit; and in such cases
Men's natures wrangle with inferior things,
Though great ones are their object. 'Tis even so.
For let our finger ache, and it endues
Our healthful members even to that sense
140 Of pain. Nay, we must think men are not gods,
Nor of them look for such observancy
As fits the bridal. Beshrew me much, Emilia,
I was—unhandsome warrior as I am—
Arraigning his unkindness with my soul;
145 But now I find I had suborned the witness
And he's indicted falsely.
        Emilia
Pray heaven it be state matters, as you think,
And no conception nor no jealous toy
Concerning you.
        Desdemona
150 Alas the day, I never gave him cause.

152 *ever*: always.
     for the cause: for some reason.
153 *for*: because.
     It: Emilia echoes her husband's
     description of the monster which is the
     personification of jealousy.

Emilia
But jealous souls will not be answered so;
They are not ever jealous for the cause,
But jealous for they're jealous. It is a monster
Begot upon itself, born on itself.
Desdemona
155 Heaven keep that monster from Othello's mind.
Emilia
Lady, amen!
Desdemona
I will go seek him. Cassio, walk here about.
If I do find him fit, I'll move your suit,
And seek to effect it to my uttermost.
Cassio
160 I humbly thank your ladyship.

                    [*Exeunt* Desdemona *and* Emilia

          Enter Bianca

161 *'Save you*: Bianca gives a familiar
     greeting—'God Save you'—to Cassio.
     What ... home: What are you doing away
     from home?
162 *How ... you*: How are you?

Bianca
'Save you, friend Cassio.
Cassio   What make you from home?
How is it with you, my most fair Bianca?
I'faith, sweet love, I was coming to your house.
Bianca
And I was going to your lodging, Cassio.

165 *a week*: It would seem that a week has
     elapsed between this scene and the previous
     one; but see p. xv.
166 *lovers' absent hours*: the hours when lovers
     are away from each other.
167 *dial*: clock.
169 *leaden ... pressed*: tortured (as a victim was
     pressed to death with heavy weights) by
     heavy thoughts.
170 *continuate*: uninterrupted.
171 *Strike off this score*: Cassio picks up 'score'
     from Bianca and uses it to mean 'debt'; in
     an inn the customer's bill—'score'—would
     be kept until he could pay—strike it off.
172 *Take ... out*: Copy this embroidery for
     me.
     whence came this: where did you get this?
173 *token*: i.e. love-token.
     friend: i.e. mistress.

165 What! Keep a week away? Seven days and nights?
Eight score eight hours? And lovers' absent hours
More tedious than the dial eight score times!
O weary reckoning!
Cassio   Pardon me, Bianca.
I have this while with leaden thoughts been pressed:
170 But I shall in a more continuate time
Strike off this score of absence. Sweet Bianca,
Take me this work out.
Bianca   O Cassio, whence came this?
This is some token from a newer friend.
To the felt absence now I feel a cause.
175 Is't come to this? Well, well.
Cassio   Go to, woman!
Throw your vile guesses in the devil's teeth
From whence you have them. You are jealous now
That this is from some mistress, some remembrance:
No, by my faith, Bianca.

Bianca   Why, whose is it?
Cassio
180 I know not, sweet. I found it in my chamber.
     I like the work well. Ere it be demanded—
     As like enough it will—I'd have it copied.
     Take it and do't, and leave me for this time.
     Bianca
     Leave you? Wherefore?
     Cassio
185 I do attend here on the general,
     And think it no addition, nor my wish,
     To have him see me womaned.
     Bianca   Why, I pray you?
     Cassio
     Not that I love you not.
     Bianca   But that you do not love me.
     I pray you, bring me on the way a little,
190 And say if I shall see you soon at night.
     Cassio
     'Tis but a little way that I can bring you,
     For I attend here: but I'll see you soon.
     Bianca
     'Tis very good: I must be circumstanced.   [*Exeunt*

186 *no addition*: not good for me.
187 *womaned*: with a woman.

193 *circumstanced*: put up with it.

Act 4

Act 4   Scene 1

Iago continues to stir up Othello's jealousy
until the Moor is completely overwhelmed
by his passion. Cassio arrives on the scene,
but he is quickly sent away for a few
moments, and Iago devises a new torment
for Othello, which he puts into operation as
soon as Cassio reappears. Whilst Othello
listens, Iago jests with Cassio about a
woman who is in love with him. The
woman is, of course, Bianca: but Othello
assumes that Desdemona is being referred
to. Just as he is swearing vengeance, he is
interrupted by an embassy from Venice.
Lodovico watches in horror as Othello
strikes his wife and humiliates her. After
Othello and Desdemona have left the stage,
Lodovico turns to Iago; and he is told that
this is the Moor's normal behaviour.

1   *Will ... so*: Iago gives the appearance of
trying to reason with Othello's
suspicion—and all the time inflames it.
3   *friend*: with overtones of 'lover'.
6   *hypocrisy against the devil*: i.e. they would be
cheating the devil if they appeared to be
sinful when in fact they were innocent.
7   *mean virtuously*: have innocent intentions.
8   *The devil ... tempts*: The devil puts a severe
strain on their virtue.
they tempt heaven: they put a serious strain
on God's understanding and forgiveness.
9   *So*: So long as.
venial: trivial human misdeed (not a mortal
sin).

16   *essence*: entity.
17   *have it very oft*: very often appear to have
it.

Scene 1

Enter Othello *and* Iago

Iago
Will you think so?
    Othello   Think so, Iago?
    Iago   What!
To kiss in private?
    Othello   An unauthorized kiss.
    Iago
Or to be naked with her friend in bed
An hour or more, not meaning any harm?
    Othello
5   Naked in bed, Iago, and not mean harm?
It is hypocrisy against the devil.
They that mean virtuously and yet do so,
The devil their virtue tempts, and they tempt
   heaven.
    Iago
So they do nothing, 'tis a venial slip.
10   But if I give my wife a handkerchief—
    Othello
What then?
    Iago
Why, then, 'tis hers, my lord, and being hers,
She may, I think, bestow't on any man.
    Othello
She is protectress of her honour too.
15   May she give that?
    Iago
Her honour is an essence that's not seen:
They have it very oft that have it not.
But for the handkerchief—

20 *o'er*: into.
21 *the raven*: This was thought to be a bird of ill omen, especially when it perched on a house whose inmates were suffering from the plague.
22 *Boding*: Promising ill.

25 *as ... abroad*: there are such villains about.
26 *importunate suit*: persistent wooing.
27 *voluntary dotage*: weakness of will.
28 *Convincèd ... them*: Conquered or seduced by them.
   cannot choose: can't help it.
29 *blab*: talk about it.

31 *unswear*: deny. Here again, lines are divided between the two speakers, as each reacts quickly to the other.

36 *belie*: tell lies about.
   Lie with her: Sleep with her—i.e. make love to her.
   fulsome: disgusting.
37-38 *confess and be hanged*: A proverbial expression which was a way of accusing someone of lying.
39 *I tremble*: Othello's emotion is physically as well as mentally overpowering. In the next few lines he struggles to control himself.
40 *invest*: clothe.
   shadowing: overwhelming.
41 *instruction*: reason.
42 *Noses, ears, and lips*: Othello may be thinking that their noses and lips may have touched in kissing, and their ears have been close together for whispering.

Othello
By heaven, I would most gladly have forgot it!
20 Thou said'st—O, it comes o'er my memory
As doth the raven o'er the infected house,
Boding to all!—he had my handkerchief.
   Iago
Ay, what of that?
   Othello   That's not so good now.
   Iago   What
If I had said, I had seen him do you wrong,
25 Or heard him say—as knaves be such abroad,
Who having by their own importunate suit
Or voluntary dotage of some mistress
Convincèd or supplied them, cannot choose
But they must blab—
   Othello   Hath he said anything?
   Iago
30 He hath, my lord; but be you well assured,
No more than he'll unswear.
   Othello   What hath he said?
   Iago
Faith, that he did—I know not what he did.
   Othello
What? What?
   Iago
Lie—
   Othello With her?
   Iago   With her, on her, what you will.
   Othello
35 Lie with her? Lie on her? We say lie on her when they belie her. Lie with her? Zounds, that's fulsome! Handkerchief—confession—handkerchief! To confess and be hanged for his labour. First to be hanged and then to confess! I tremble at it. Nature would not
40 invest herself in such shadowing passion without some instruction. It is not words that shakes me thus! Pish! Noses, ears, and lips! Is't possible?—Confess? Handkerchief! O devil!

   He falls

Iago
Work on,
45 My medicine, work! Thus credulous fools are
    caught,
And many worthy and chaste dames even thus,
All guiltless, meet reproach. What ho, my lord!
My lord, I say! Othello!

Enter Cassio

                                How now, Cassio!
Cassio
What's the matter?
Iago
50 My lord is fallen into an epilepsy.
This is his second fit: he had one yesterday.
Cassio
Rub him about the temples.
Iago   No, forbear,
The lethargy must have his quiet course.
If not, he foams at mouth; and by and by
55 Breaks out to savage madness. Look, he stirs.
Do you withdraw yourself a little while:
He will recover straight. When he is gone,
I would on great occasion speak with you.
                                    [*Exit* Cassio
How is it, general. Have you not hurt your head?
Othello
60 Dost thou mock me?
Iago   I mock you? No, by heaven!
Would you would bear your fortune like a man!
Othello
A hornèd man's a monster and a beast.
Iago
There's many a beast then in a populous city,
And many a civil monster.
Othello
65 Did he confess it?
Iago   Good sir, be a man.
Think every bearded fellow that's but yoked
May draw with you. There's millions now alive
That nightly lie in those unproper beds
Which they dare swear peculiar. Your case is better.
70 O, 'tis the spite of hell, the fiend's arch-mock,

47 *meet reproach*: are shamed.

50 *epilepsy*: epileptic fit; but this—and the information that Othello 'had one yesterday'—is probably an invention of Iago's, designed to mislead Cassio.

53 *lethargy*: coma.
    his quiet course: its way undisturbed.

57 *When he is gone*: When the fit is over.
58 *great occasion*: a serious matter.

59 *hurt your head*: Iago can ask the question with apparent innocence, concerned that Othello may have hurt himself in falling; but Othello *hears* a mocking reference to the cuckold's horns.
61 *Would*: I wish.
    fortune: i.e. your bad luck in having a faithless wife.

64 *civil*: civilized.
66 *bearded fellow*: adult male.
    yoked: married; *and* (of oxen) harnessed to a plough.
67 *draw*: pull the plough.
68 *unproper beds*: beds which their wives have shared with other men.
69 *peculiar*: their own alone.
    Your ... better: Othello is luckier than those men who do not know they have been cuckolded.
70 *arch-mock*: supreme mockery.

71 *lip*: kiss.
   wanton: faithless woman.
   secure: free from suspicion.
72 *let me know*: I would rather know.
73 *what I am*: i.e. a cuckold.
   what shall be: what must be done.

75 Keep within the bounds of patience (a 'list' was a barrier).

78 *shifted him away*: got rid of him.
79 *laid good 'scuse*: made a good excuse.
   ecstasy: frenzied behaviour.
80 *anon*: immediately.
81 *encave*: conceal.
82 *fleers*: mocks.
   gibes: jeers.
   notable: obvious.
83 *dwell ... face*: show all over his face.

86 *cope*: copulate with.
88 *all ... spleen*: utterly consumed with passion (which was thought to reside in the spleen).

90 *cunning*: careful.

92 *keep time*: be controlled.

93 *Now ... Bianca*: Now I will talk to Cassio about Bianca; Iago takes the audience into his confidence.
94 *housewife*: hussy.
   her desires: sexual desires—her body.

101 *unbookish*: uneducated.
    construe: interpret; the image is that of the poor scholar who cannot translate his lesson.

104 *addition*: title.
105 *Whose want*: The lack of which.

To lip a wanton in a secure couch,
And to suppose her chaste! No, let me know;
And knowing what I am, I know what shall be.

Othello
O, thou art wise, 'tis certain.

Iago   Stand you awhile apart;
75 Confine yourself but in a patient list.
Whilst you were here, o'erwhelmèd with your grief—
A passion most unsuiting such a man—
Cassio came hither. I shifted him away
And laid good 'scuse upon your ecstasy;
80 Bade him anon return and here speak with me,
The which he promised. Do but encave yourself,
And mark the fleers, the gibes, and notable scorns
That dwell in every region of his face.
For I will make him tell the tale anew,
85 Where, how, how oft, how long ago, and when
He hath, and is again, to cope your wife.
I say, but mark his gesture. Marry, patience!
Or I shall say you're all in all in spleen
And nothing of a man.

Othello   Dost thou hear, Iago?
90 I will be found most cunning in my patience,
But—dost thou hear?—most bloody.

Iago   That's not amiss,
But yet keep time in all. Will you withdraw?

                                    [Othello *retires*
Now will I question Cassio of Bianca,
A housewife, that by selling her desires
95 Buys herself bread and clothes. It is a creature
That dotes on Cassio—as 'tis the strumpet's plague
To beguile many and be beguiled by one.
He, when he hears of her, cannot refrain
From the excess of laughter. Here he comes.

Enter Cassio

100 As he shall smile, Othello shall go mad;
And his unbookish jealousy must construe
Poor Cassio's smiles, gestures, and light behaviour
Quite in the wrong. How do you now, lieutenant?

Cassio
The worser that you give me the addition
105 Whose want even kills me.

108 *caitiff*: wretch (affectionate).

116 *gives it out*: tells people.

119 *triumph*: gloat; conquerors in ancient Rome were given a ceremonial procession of triumph—and this may account for the reference to Cassio as 'Roman'.
120 *customer*: whore.
120-1 *bear ... wit*: give me credit for some sense.
121 *unwholesome*: unhealthy.
123 *So, so, so*: The call of a huntsman encouraging his hounds.
124 *cry*: rumour; *and* the cry from hounds who have picked up the scent of their quarry.
125 *say true*: not really.

127 *scored*: wounded, marked.

129 *flattery*: i.e. she flatters herself.

Iago
Ply Desdemona well and you are sure on't.
Now if this suit lay in Bianca's power,
How quickly should you speed!
Cassio   Alas, poor caitiff!
Othello
[*Aside*] Look, how he laughs already!
Iago
110 I never knew a woman love man so.
Cassio
Alas, poor rogue! I think i'faith she loves me.
Othello
[*Aside*] Now he denies it faintly, and laughs it out.
Iago
Do you hear, Cassio?
Othello
[*Aside*] Now he importunes him to tell it o'er.
115 Go to, well said, well said!
Iago
She gives it out that you shall marry her.
Do you intend it?
Cassio
Ha, ha, ha!
Othello
[*Aside*] Do you triumph, Roman? Do you triumph?
Cassio
120 I marry her! What! A customer! Prithee bear some charity to my wit: do not think it so unwholesome. Ha, ha, ha!
Othello
[*Aside*] So, so, so, so: they laugh that win.
Iago
Faith, the cry goes that you shall marry her.
Cassio
125 Prithee, say true.
Iago
I am a very villain else.
Othello
[*Aside*] Have you scored me? Well.
Cassio
This is the monkey's own giving out. She is persuaded I will marry her out of her own love and flattery,
130 not out of my promise.

Othello

[*Aside*] Iago beckons me. Now he begins the story.

Cassio

She was here even now. She haunts me in every place. I was the other day talking on the sea-bank with certain Venetians, and thither comes the bauble and, by this hand, falls me thus about my neck.

Othello

[*Aside*] Crying 'O dear Cassio!' as it were. His gesture imports it.

Cassio

So hangs and lolls and weeps upon me, so hales and pulls me. Ha, ha, ha!

Othello

[*Aside*] Now she tells how she plucked him to my chamber. O, I see that nose of yours, but not that dog I shall throw it to!

Cassio

Well, I must leave her company.

Iago

Before me! Look where she comes.

Cassio

'Tis such another fitchew! Marry, a perfumed one!

Enter Bianca

What do you mean by this haunting of me?

Bianca

Let the devil and his dam haunt you! What did you mean by that same handkerchief you gave me even now? I was a fine fool to take it. I must take out the work! A likely piece of work, that you should find it in your chamber, and not know who left it there! This is some minx's token, and I must take out the work? There, give it your hobby-horse, wheresoever you had it. I'll take out no work on't.

Cassio

How now, my sweet Bianca! How now, how now!

Othello

[*Aside*] By heaven, that should be my handkerchief!

Bianca

If you'll come to supper tonight, you may. If you will not, come when you are next prepared for.

[*Exit*

Glossary (left margin):

132 *even now*: just now.

134 *bauble*: plaything.
135 *falls ... neck*: throws her arms round my neck.

137 *imports*: suggests.

138 *hales*: tugs.

140 *plucked*: drew.
141-2 *that nose*: Othello thinks of cutting off Cassio's nose and throwing it to a dog.
143 *leave her company*: stop seeing her.
144 *Before me*: An exclamation of surprise (= Upon my soul!).
145 *such another*: no other than.
fitchew: polecat, a creature noted for its smell when sexually aroused.
perfumed: prostitutes were often highly-scented.

147 *the devil and his dam*: A proverbial expression.

149 *take out*: copy.
150 *piece of work*: story.

153 *hobby-horse*: whore—something that any man can ride for fun.

156 *should*: must.

158 *next prepared for*: next time you feel like it.

Iago
After her, after her!

Cassio

160 Faith I must: she'll rail in the street else.

Iago
Will you sup there?

Cassio
Faith, I intend to.

Iago
Well, I may chance to see you: for I would very fain speak with you.

Cassio

165 Prithee come, will you?

Iago
Go to! Say no more.   [*Exit* Cassio

Othello
[*Coming forward*] How shall I murder him, Iago?

Iago
Did you perceive how he laughed at his vice?

Othello
O Iago!

Iago

170 And did you see the handkerchief?

Othello
Was that mine?

Iago
Yours, by this hand! And to see how he prizes the foolish woman your wife: she gave it him, and he hath giv'n it his whore.

Othello

175 I would have him nine years a-killing!—A fine woman, a fair woman, a sweet woman!

Iago
Nay, you must forget that.

Othello
Ay, let her rot and perish, and be damned tonight, for she shall not live! No, my heart is turned to stone: I
180 strike it, and it hurts my hand. —O, the world hath not a sweeter creature! She might lie by an emperor's side and command him tasks.

Iago
Nay, that's not your way.

Othello
Hang her! I do but say what she is: so delicate with her

160 *rail*: shout.
    else: otherwise.

163 *very fain*: very much like to.

166 *Go to*: Off you go.

172 *by this hand*: I swear it.

175 *a-killing*: dying a slow death.

183 You should not be thinking like this; Iago turns Othello's thoughts away from his love.

185 needle, an admirable musician! O she will sing the savageness out of a bear! Of so high and plenteous wit and invention!

Iago

She's the worse for all this.

Othello

O a thousand, thousand times!—And then of so gentle a
190 condition.

Iago

Ay, too gentle.

Othello

Nay, that's certain—but yet the pity of it, Iago! O Iago, the pity of it, Iago!

Iago

If you are so fond over her iniquity, give her patent to
195 offend, for if it touch not you, it comes near nobody.

Othello

I will chop her into messes! Cuckold me!

Iago

O, 'tis foul in her!

Othello

With mine officer!

Iago

That's fouler.

Othello

200 Get me some poison, Iago, this night. I'll not expostulate with her, lest her body and beauty unprovide my mind again—this night, Iago.

Iago

Do it not with poison; strangle her in her bed, even the bed she hath contaminated.

Othello

205 Good, good! The justice of it pleases; very good!

Iago

And for Cassio, let me be his undertaker. You shall hear more by midnight.

Othello

Excellent good!

Trumpet sounds

What trumpet is that same?

Iago

I warrant, something from Venice.

187 *invention*: imagination.

189 *so gentle a condition*: well-bred; *and* with such a gentle nature.

191 *too gentle*: i.e. too yielding.

194 *fond over*: foolish about.
    patent: licence.
195 *if ... nobody*: if it doesn't hurt you, it won't affect anyone else.
196 *messes*: little bits of meat.

201 *expostulate*: argue.
202 *unprovide*: weaken.

206 *be his undertaker*: look after him.

208 *Excellent good*: Blank verse and a degree of formality return to the scene.

Enter Lodovico, Desdemona, *and*
Attendants

                          'Tis Lodovico,
210 Come from the Duke; and see, your wife is with
him.

Lodovico
God save you, worthy general!

Othello   With all my heart, sir.

Lodovico
The Duke and senators of Venice greet you.

He gives him a letter

Othello
I kiss the instrument of their pleasures.

He reads the letter

Desdemona
And what's the news, good cousin Lodovico?

Iago
215 I am very glad to see you, signor:
Welcome to Cyprus.

Lodovico
I thank you. How does lieutenant Cassio?

Iago
Lives, sir.

Desdemona
Cousin, there's fallen between him and my lord
220 An unkind breach; but you shall make all well.

Othello
Are you sure of that?

Desdemona
My lord?

Othello
'This fail you not to do, as you will'—

Lodovico
He did not call: he's busy in the paper.
225 Is there division 'twixt my lord and Cassio?

Desdemona
A most unhappy one; I would do much
T'atone them, for the love I bear to Cassio.

Othello
Fire and brimstone!

Desdemona
My lord?

213 Othello shows his respect to the state by kissing the letter from Venice.

214 *cousin*: a polite form of address which did not necessarily indicate relationship.

220 *breach*: quarrel.

224 *in the paper*: reading the letter.
225 *division*: difference of opinion.

227 *atone*: bring them together.

228 Othello reacts to Desdemona's words, not to the letter from Venice.

Othello

230 Are you wise?

Desdemona

What, is he angry?

Lodovico   Maybe the letter moved him.
For, as I think, they do command him home,
Deputing Cassio in his government.

Desdemona

By my troth, I am glad on't.

Othello   Indeed!

Desdemona   My lord?

Othello

235 I am glad to see you mad.

Desdemona   Why, sweet Othello!

Othello

Devil!

He strikes her

Desdemona

I have not deserved this.

Lodovico

My lord, this would not be believed in Venice,
Though I should swear I saw't. 'Tis very much.

240 Make her amends; she weeps.

Othello   O devil, devil!
If that the earth could teem with woman's tears,
Each drop she falls would prove a crocodile.
Out of my sight!

Desdemona   I will not stay to offend you.

Lodovico

Truly an obedient lady.

245 I do beseech your lordship call her back.

Othello

Mistress!

Desdemona

My lord!

Othello

What would you with her, sir?

Lodovico

Who? I, my lord?

Othello

250 Ay, you did wish that I would make her turn.
Sir, she can turn, and turn, and yet go on,

241-2 'If life were to be bred from the earth whenever women weep, each of her tears would produce a crocodile'; it was thought that the crocodile shed false tears to deceive its prey.
241 *teem*: give birth.
242 *falls*: sheds.

246 *Mistress*: Othello calls to Desdemona as though she were a prostitute in a brothel, where Lodovico is the customer.

250 *turn*: come back.
251 *turn*: turn on her back, change her mind, *and* change her loyalty.

254 *proceed ... tears*: carry on crying.
255 *well-painted passion*: a good show of grief.

257 *mandate*: command.
258 *avaunt*: get out of my sight.

259 *place*: position.
260 *sup*: eat supper.
261 *Goats and monkeys*: Lecherous beasts;
     Othello's passion breaks through his self-
     control.

262 *full*: wise.
263 *all-in-all sufficient*: totally competent.
264 *solid*: steady.
265 *shot of accident*: cannon shot of fortune.
     dart of chance: arrow of fate.

267 *his wits safe*: in his right mind.
     light of brain: going insane.
268-9 *He's ... were*: Iago does not wish to be
     fully understood, and his cryptic comment
     is not easily paraphrased.
268 *that*: what.
     breathe my censure: give my opinion.
269 *might be*: i.e. mad.
270 *would*: wish; perhaps Iago is hoping that
     Othello will become mad.

272 *Is ... use*: Does he often do this?
273 *work ... blood*: anger him.
274 *new-create*: initiate.

277 *courses*: actions.
     denote: reveal.

And turn again. And she can weep, sir, weep.
And she's obedient; as you say, obedient,
Very obedient—proceed you in your tears—
255 Concerning this, sir—O, well-painted passion!—
I am commanded home—get you away!
I'll send for you anon. —Sir, I obey the mandate,
And will return to Venice. —Hence, avaunt!
                              [*Exit* Desdemona
Cassio shall have my place. And sir, tonight
260 I do entreat that we may sup together.
You are welcome, sir, to Cyprus. Goats and
     monkeys!
                                        [*Exit*

Lodovico
Is this the noble Moor, whom our full senate
Call all-in-all sufficient? Is this the nature
Whom passion could not shake? Whose solid virtue
265 The shot of accident nor dart of chance
Could neither graze nor pierce?
Iago   He is much changed.
Lodovico
Are his wits safe? Is he not light of brain?
Iago
He's that he is: I may not breathe my censure
What he might be. If what he might he is not,
270 I would to heaven he were.
Lodovico   What! Strike his wife!
Iago
Faith, that was not so well: yet would I knew
That stroke would prove the worst!
Lodovico   Is it his use?
Or did the letters work upon his blood
And new-create this fault?
Iago   Alas, alas!
275 It is not honesty in me to speak
What I have seen and known. You shall observe
     him,
And his own courses will denote him so,
That I may save my speech. Do but go after,
And mark how he continues.
Lodovico
280 I am sorry that I am deceived in him.
                                      [*Exeunt*

Act 4   Scene 2

Othello questions Emilia about her mistress, speaking to her as though she were the keeper of a brothel; but he refuses to believe what he is told, and confronts Desdemona with his suspicions. She is quite bewildered by his passionate outburst, and when Emilia returns, accompanied by Iago, Desdemona is driven to ask Iago for comfort and reassurance in her trouble. As usual, Iago promises to help; and the two women leave for supper. Now Roderigo returns, once again reproaching Iago for unfair dealings—and once again Iago convinces him that everything is going according to plan.

5 *breath made up*: was spoken.

11 *durst*: dare.
   honest: chaste.
12 *at stake*: at risk.
   other: otherwise.
13 *Remove your thought*: Forget it.
15 *the serpent's curse*: the curse that God put upon the snake (the devil) who deceived Eve in the Garden of Eden (*Genesis* 3: 14–15).

19 *she's a simple bawd*: it would be a poor bawd (= keeper of a brothel; Othello insists on thinking of Desdemona as a prostitute).
21 *closet, lock and key*: cupboard securely fastened.

Scene 2

Enter Othello *and* Emilia

Othello
You have seen nothing then?
    Emilia
Nor ever heard, nor ever did suspect.
    Othello
Yes, you have seen Cassio and she together.
    Emilia
But then I saw no harm; and then I heard
5 Each syllable that breath made up between them.
    Othello
What, did they never whisper?
    Emilia   Never, my lord.
    Othello
Nor send you o'th'way?
    Emilia   Never.
    Othello
To fetch her fan, her gloves, her mask, nor nothing?
    Emilia
Never, my lord.
    Othello
10 That's strange.
    Emilia
I durst, my lord, to wager she is honest,
Lay down my soul at stake. If you think other,
Remove your thought: it doth abuse your bosom.
If any wretch have put this in your head,
15 Let heaven requite it with the serpent's curse!
For if she be not honest, chaste, and true,
There's no man happy. The purest of their wives
Is foul as slander.
    Othello   Bid her come hither: go!
                                 [*Exit* Emilia
She says enough; yet she's a simple bawd
20 That cannot say as much. This is a subtle whore,
A closet, lock and key, of villainous secrets;
And yet she'll kneel and pray—I have seen her do't.

Enter Desdemona *and* Emilia

    Desdemona
My lord, what is your will?

Othello   Pray, chuck, come hither.
Desdemona
What is your pleasure?
Othello   Let me see your eyes.
25 Look in my face.
Desdemona   What horrible fancy's this?
Othello
[*To* Emilia]
Some of your function, mistress,
Leave procreants alone and shut the door;
Cough or cry 'hem' if anybody come.
Your mystery, your mystery! Nay, dispatch!
                                    [*Exit* Emilia

Desdemona
30 Upon my knees, what doth your speech import?
I understand a fury in your words,
But not the words.
Othello   Why, what art thou?
Desdemona
Your wife, my lord; your true and loyal wife.
Othello
Come, swear it; damn thyself;
35 Lest being like one of heaven, the devils themselves
Should fear to seize thee. Therefore be double-
    damned:
Swear thou art honest.
Desdemona   Heaven doth truly know it.
Othello
Heaven truly knows that thou art false as hell.
Desdemona
To whom, my lord? With whom? How am I false?
Othello
40 Ah, Desdemon! Away, away, away!
Desdemona
Alas, the heavy day! Why do you weep?
Am I the motive of these tears, my lord?
If haply you my father do suspect
An instrument of this your calling back,
45 Lay not your blame on me. If you have lost him,
I have lost him too.
Othello   Had it pleased heaven
To try me with affliction, had they rained
All kind of sores and shames on my bare head,
Steeped me in poverty to the very lips,

26 *of your function*: with your job (i.e. as brothel-keeper).
27 *procreants*: those engaged in procreation.
29 *mystery*: do your job.
   dispatch: get on with it.

35 *like one of heaven*: like an angel.

41 *heavy*: sorrowful.
42 *motive*: cause.
43-4 If perhaps you think my father was responsible for your being recalled to Venice.
45 *him*: his favour.

46 *Had it*: If it had.
47 *try*: test.

49 *Steeped*: Submerged.

50 *utmost*: all.

53–4 Othello sees himself as an object of contempt, pointed to (in mockery) as the number on a dial is pointed to by the hand of the clock, which moves so slowly that it seems to be unmoving.

56 *garnered up my heart*: stored up all my love; the image is from farming: corn is 'garnered up' at harvest-time.

57 *Where*: In loving Desdemona; if Othello cannot continue to love her, he cannot go on living.

58 *fountain*: source.
 current: stream.

60 *cistern*: pond.

61 *knot and gender*: twine together and breed.
 Turn ... there: Look pale (with horror).

62 *cherubin*: angel; at the thought of Desdemona's transformation (from a pure spring of love to a slimy pond), the goddess Patience—personified as a young and innocent angel—should turn pale and look fierce.

64 *esteems*: considers.

65 *shambles*: butchers' slaughterhouse.

66 *quicken even with blowing*: hatch as soon as the eggs are laid.

69 *what ... committed*: 'What sin have I, in all innocence, been guilty of'; but the sin most readily associated with the verb 'commit' is adultery (as in the commandment 'Thou shalt not commit adultery), and Othello is quick to make the association.

72 *commoner*: whore—one whose sexual favours are common to all.

73–4 Othello feels that his cheeks would burn with such shame that all modesty would be destroyed; 'forges' are blacksmiths' furnaces.

76 *it*: i.e. the smell of Desdemona's sin.
 winks: refuses to see; the goddess of the moon was also the goddess of chastity.

78 *hollow mine of earth*: the depths—bowels—of the earth.

82 *vessel*: i.e. her body; the expression is biblical.

50 Given to captivity me and my utmost hopes,
 I should have found in some place of my soul
 A drop of patience. But alas, to make me
 A fixèd figure for the time of scorn
 To point his slow unmoving finger at!
55 Yet could I bear that too, well, very well:
 But there where I have garnered up my heart,
 Where either I must live, or bear no life,
 The fountain from the which my current runs,
 Or else dries up—to be discarded thence
60 Or keep it as a cistern for foul toads
 To knot and gender in! Turn thy complexion there,
 Patience, thou young and rose-lipped cherubin,
 Ay, there look grim as hell!

Desdemona
 I hope my noble lord esteems me honest.

Othello
65 O ay! As summer flies are in the shambles,
 That quicken even with blowing, O thou weed,
 Who art so lovely fair, and smell'st so sweet
 That the sense aches at thee, would thou hadst ne'er
  been born!

Desdemona
 Alas, what ignorant sin have I committed?

Othello
70 Was this fair paper, this most goodly book,
 Made to write 'whore' upon? What committed!
 Committed? O thou public commoner!
 I should make very forges of my cheeks,
 That would to cinders burn up modesty,
75 Did I but speak thy deeds. What committed?
 Heaven stops the nose at it, and the moon winks;
 The bawdy wind, that kisses all it meets,
 Is hushed within the hollow mine of earth
 And will not hear it. What committed?
80 Impudent strumpet!

Desdemona   By heaven, you do me wrong.

Othello
 Are you not a strumpet?

Desdemona   No, as I am a Christian.
 If to preserve this vessel for my lord
 From any other foul unlawful touch,
 Be not to be a strumpet, I am none.

87 *cry you mercy*: beg your pardon.
88 *took you for*: mistook you for.

90 *Saint Peter*: The saint who guards the
    gates of heaven.
91 *Keep the gate of hell*: Othello returns to the
    language of the brothel.

92 *done our course*: finished what we had to
    do.
93 *turn the key*: unlock the door (Emilia was
    told to close the door at line 27).
    keep our counsel: keep quiet about what we
    have been doing.
94 *conceive*: imagine.

96 *half asleep*: Desdemona is dazed by
    Othello's words.

103 *go by water*: be conveyed by tears.

106 *meet*: fitting; Desdemona is perhaps
     bitterly ironical, rather than meekly
     submissive.
107 *How ... behaved*: What have I done?
107-8 *that ... misuse*: to give him any reason
       for misinterpreting my smallest fault.

Othello
85 What! Not a whore?
    Desdemona   No, as I shall be saved.
    Othello
    Is't possible?
    Desdemona
    O heaven forgive us!
    Othello   I cry you mercy then:
    I took you for that cunning whore of Venice
    That married with Othello. [*Calling*] You, mistress,
90 That have the office opposite to Saint Peter
    And keep the gate of hell!

              Enter Emilia
                      You, you, ay, you!
    We have done our course: there's money for your
       pains.
    I pray you turn the key, and keep our counsel.   [*Exit*
    Emilia
    Alas, what does this gentleman conceive?
95 How do you, madam? How do you, my good lady?
    Desdemona
    Faith, half asleep.
    Emilia
    Good madam, what's the matter with my lord?
    Desdemona
    With who?
    Emilia
    Why, with my lord, madam.
    Desdemona
100 Who is thy lord?
    Emilia   He that is yours, sweet lady.
    Desdemona
    I have none. Do not talk to me, Emilia:
    I cannot weep; nor answers have I none,
    But what should go by water. Prithee, tonight
    Lay on my bed my wedding sheets, remember,
105 And call thy husband hither.
    Emilia   Here's a change indeed!
                                            [*Exit*
    Desdemona
    'Tis meet I should be used so, very meet.
    How have I been behaved, that he might stick
    The smallest opinion on my least misuse?

Enter Emilia *and* Iago

Iago
What is your pleasure, madam? How is't with you?

Desdemona
110   I cannot tell: those that do teach young babes
Do it with gentle means and easy tasks:
He might have chid me so, for, in good faith,
I am a child to chiding.

Iago   What is the matter, lady?

Emilia
Alas, Iago, my lord hath so bewhored her,
115   Thrown such despite and heavy terms upon her
As true heart cannot bear.

Desdemona
Am I that name, Iago?

Iago   What name, fair lady?

Desdemona
Such as she said my lord did say I was.

Emilia
He called her whore: a beggar in his drink
120   Could not have laid such terms upon his callet.

Iago
Why did he so?

Desdemona
I do not know: I am sure I am none such.

Iago
Do not weep, do not weep. Alas the day!

Emilia
Hath she forsook so many noble matches,
125   Her father, and her country, all her friends,
To be called whore? Would it not make one weep?

Desdemona
It is my wretched fortune.

Iago   Beshrew him for't!
How comes this trick upon him?

Desdemona   Nay, heaven doth know.

Emilia
I will be hanged if some eternal villain,
130   Some busy and insinuating rogue,
Some cogging, cozening slave, to get some office,
Have not devised this slander; I'll be hanged else.

---

113   *a child to chiding*: unaccustomed to being scolded.

114   *bewhored her*: called her a whore.
115   *despite and heavy terms*: contempt and insults.

119   *in his drink*: drunken.
120   *laid such terms*: used such language.
       callet: slut.

124   *forsook*: given up.

128   *How ... him*: Where did he get this idea from?
129   *eternal*: damned (eternally); without knowing, Emilia describes her husband.
130   *busy*: interfering.
131   *cogging*: lying.
       cozening: cheating.
       to get some office: for some reason, *or* to get some job out of it; Emilia is very close to the truth.

133 *impossible*: Iago listens to the descriptions of his villainy whilst denying its possibility.

135 *A halter pardon him*: May he be hanged.
136 *keeps her company*: is her lover.

137 *form*: appearance.
what likelihood: what did he look like?

139 *scurvy*: miserable.
140 *companions*: villains.
thou'dst: thou wouldest; i.e. I wish you would.
unfold: reveal.

143 *within door*: quietly.

144 *squire*: fellow.
145 *turned ... without*: fooled you (as though by making him wear his coat inside out).
146 *suspect me*: i.e. of infidelity.

151-8 Desdemona prays that she may lose all peace of body and soul if she ever sinned or sins against Othello.
151 *will*: wishes.
trespass: offend.
152 *discourse of thought*: what I thought.
154 *Delighted them*: Enjoyed.

158 *Comfort forswear me*: May all happiness forsake me.
159 *defeat*: destroy.

161 *It does abhor me*: I am disgusted.

162-3 Not for all the empty pleasures of the world ('the world's mass of vanity') would I do the deed which would earn me such a title ('addition').
164 *but his humour*: only his mood.
165 *does him offence*: annoys him.
166 *chide with you*: quarrel with you.

Iago
Fie, there is no such man! It is impossible.
Desdemona
If any such there be, heaven pardon him.
Emilia
135   A halter pardon him and hell gnaw his bones!
Why should he call her whore? Who keeps her
   company?
What place, what time, what form, what likelihood?
The Moor's abused by some most villainous knave,
Some base notorious knave, some scurvy fellow.
140   O heaven, that such companions thou'dst unfold,
And put in every honest hand a whip
To lash the rascals naked through the world,
Even from the east to th'west!
Iago   Speak within door.
Emilia
O fie upon them! Some such squire he was
145   That turned your wit the seamy side without
And made you to suspect me with the Moor.
Iago
You are a fool, go to.
Desdemona   O good Iago,
What shall I do to win my lord again?
Good friend, go to him; for, by this light of heaven,
150   I know not how I lost him. Here I kneel:
If e'er my will did trespass 'gainst his love,
Either in discourse of thought or actual deed;
Or that mine eyes, mine ears, or any sense
Delighted them in any other form;
155   Or that I do not yet, and ever did,
And ever will—though he do shake me off
To beggarly divorcement—love him dearly,
Comfort forswear me! Unkindness may do much,
And his unkindness may defeat my life,
160   But never taint my love. I cannot say 'whore':
It does abhor me now I speak the word;
To do the act that might the addition earn
Not the world's mass of vanity could make me.
Iago
I pray you, be content: 'tis but his humour;
165   The business of the state does him offence,
And he does chide with you.

167 *no other*: nothing else.

168 *these instruments*: probably trumpet calls.
169 *stay the meat*: await the meal.

171 A prose section—more relaxed than the previous taut verse—ends the scene.

174 *daff'st ... device*: put me off with some excuse; *daff* was a word usually applied to the taking off of clothes.
176 *conveniency*: opportunity.

178 *put up*: endure.

182 *no kin together*: bear no relation to each other.

183 *charge*: accuse.

184-5 *I have ... means*: Ruined myself financially.
186 *half*: easily.
votarist: nun.

188 *comforts*: encouragement.
sudden respect: immediate attention.

193 *fopped*: fooled.

Desdemona
If 'twere no other—
    Iago   It is so, I warrant,
Hark how these instruments summon to supper!
The messengers of Venice stay the meat.
170 Go in, and weep not; all things shall be well.
                [Exeunt Desdemona *and* Emilia

      Enter Roderigo

How now, Roderigo?
    Roderigo
I do not find that thou deal'st justly with me.
    Iago
What in the contrary?
    Roderigo
Every day thou daff'st me with some device, Iago, and
175 rather, as it seems to me now, keep'st from me all
conveniency, than suppliest me with the least
advantage of hope. I will indeed no longer endure it.
Nor am I yet persuaded to put up in peace what already
I have foolishly suffered.
    Iago
180 Will you hear me, Roderigo?
    Roderigo
Faith, I have heard too much; for your words and
performances are no kin together.
    Iago
You charge me most unjustly.
    Roderigo
With naught but truth. I have wasted myself out of my
185 means. The jewels you have had from me to deliver to
Desdemona would half have corrupted a votarist. You
have told me she hath received them, and returned me
expectations and comforts of sudden respect and
acquaintance, but I find none.
    Iago
190 Well, go to; very well.
    Roderigo
Very well, go to! I cannot go to, man, nor 'tis not very
well. Nay, I think it is scurvy and begin to find myself
fopped in it.
    Iago
Very well.

197   *solicitation*: courtship.
198   *seek satisfaction*: be revenged (i.e. by challenging him to a duel).

200–1   *I protest ... doing*: I promise I shall do.

202   *mettle*: spirit.
203   *build ... opinion*: think better of you.
204–5   *taken ... exception*: made a very reasonable objection.
205   *protest*: declare.
206   *directly ... affair*: honestly in your interests.
207   It doesn't look that way.

214   *engines for my life*: plots against my life.

216   *compass*: possibility.

221   *he goes into Mauritania*: This is a quick invention of Iago's, to make Roderigo think that Desdemona will be completely lost to him; Mauritania was part of western Africa.
222   *abode*: stay (in Cyprus).
         lingered: delayed.
224   *determinate*: certain.

Roderigo
195 I tell you, 'tis not very well. I will make myself known to Desdemona. If she will return me my jewels, I will give over my suit and repent my unlawful solicitation. If not, assure yourself I will seek satisfaction of you.

Iago
You have said now.

Roderigo
200 Ay, and said nothing but what I protest intendment of doing.

Iago
Why, now I see there's mettle in thee; and even from this instant do build on thee a better opinion than ever before. Give me thy hand, Roderigo. Thou hast taken
205 against me a most just exception; but yet I protest I have dealt most directly in thy affair.

Roderigo
It hath not appeared.

Iago
I grant indeed it hath not appeared; and your suspicion is not without wit and judgement. But, Roderigo, if
210 thou hast that in thee indeed, which I have greater reason to believe now than ever—I mean purpose, courage, and valour—this night show it. If thou the next night following enjoy not Desdemona, take me from this world with treachery, and devise engines for
215 my life.

Roderigo
Well, what is it? Is it within reason and compass?

Iago
Sir, there is especial commission come from Venice to depute Cassio in Othello's place.

Roderigo
Is that true? Why, then Othello and Desdemona return
220 again to Venice?

Iago
O, no: he goes into Mauritania and takes away with him the fair Desdemona, unless his abode be lingered here by some accident: wherein none can be so determinate as the removing of Cassio.

Roderigo
225 How do you mean 'removing' of him?

Iago

Why, by making him uncapable of Othello's place—knocking out his brains.

Roderigo

And that you would have me to do?

Iago

Ay, if you dare do yourself a profit and a right. He sups 230 tonight with a harlotry; and thither will I go to him. He knows not yet of his honourable fortune. If you will watch his going thence—which I will fashion to fall out between twelve and one—you may take him at your pleasure. I will be near to second your 235 attempt, and he shall fall between us. Come, stand not amazed at it, but go along with me. I will show you such a necessity in his death that you shall think yourself bound to put it on him. It is now high supper-time and the night grows to waste. About it!

Roderigo

240 I will hear further reason for this.

Iago

And you shall be satisfied.   [*Exeunt*

Scene 3

Enter Othello, Lodovico, Desdemona, Emilia, *and* Attendants

Lodovico

I do beseech you, sir, trouble yourself no further.

Othello

O pardon me: 'twill do me good to walk.

Lodovico

Madam, good night. I humbly thank your ladyship.

Desdemona

Your honour is most welcome.

Othello   Will you walk, sir?

5 O Desdemona!

Desdemona

My lord?

Othello

Get you to bed on th'instant. I will be returned forthwith. Dismiss your attendant there. Look't be done.

---

228 *you would have me do*: Roderigo has come to realize that Iago will not do his own dirty work.
229 *a profit ... right*: some good, which you deserve.
230 *harlotry*: little whore.
231 *his honourable fortune*: i.e. that he has been made Othello's deputy in Cyprus.
232 *going thence*: leaving there.
233 *fashion*: organize.
     fall out: take place.
234 *second*: support.
237 *necessity in*: need for.
238 *put it on him*: bring about his death.
     high: fully.
239 *grows to waste*: is getting late.
     About it: Get on with it.

Act 4   Scene 3

Othello walks home with his guest; whilst Desdemona prepares for bed. She is sad; and recalls an old song of her youth; she talks to Emilia about marriage; revealing her own innocent ignorance. The mood of the scene is subdued: tears are never very far away.

7 *on th'instant*: at once.
8 *forthwith*: immediately.
   Dismiss: Usually the maid would stay with her mistress until the husband was ready for bed.

Desdemona   I will, my lord.

[*Exeunt* Othello, Lodovico, *and* Attendants

Emilia

10   How goes it now? He looks gentler than he did.

Desdemona

He says he will return incontinent.

He hath commanded me to go to bed,

And bade me to dismiss you.

Emilia   Dismiss me?

Desdemona

It was his bidding: therefore, good Emilia,

15   Give me my nightly wearing, and adieu.

We must not now displease him.

Emilia

I would you had never seen him.

Desdemona

So would not I: my love doth so approve him

That even his stubbornness, his checks, his frowns—

20   Prithee, unpin me—have grace and favour in them.

Emilia

I have laid those sheets you bade me on the bed.

Desdemona

All's one. Good faith, how foolish are our minds!

If I do die before thee, prithee shroud me

In one of those same sheets.

Emilia   Come, come, you talk.

Desdemona

25   My mother had a maid called Barbary:

She was in love: and he she loved proved mad

And did forsake her. She had a song of 'Willow';

An old thing 'twas; but it expressed her fortune,

And she died singing it. That song tonight

30   Will not go from my mind: I have much to do

But to go hang my head all at one side,

And sing it like poor Barbary—prithee, dispatch.

Emilia

Shall I go fetch your night-gown?

Desdemona   No, unpin me here.

This Lodovico is a proper man.

Emilia

35   A very handsome man.

Desdemona   He speaks well.

Emilia

I know a lady in Venice would have walked bare-foot

---

11   *incontinent*: straight away.

15   *nightly wearing*: night clothes.
16   Desdemona is frightened.

18   *So ... I*: That is not my wish.
      approve: value; Desdemona's love has not changed, despite Othello's harsh words.
19   *checks*: rebukes.

21   *those sheets*: i.e. the wedding sheets.
22   *All's one*: It doesn't matter; Desdemona seems to have forgotten the romantic hope that she could reconcile Othello.
23   *shroud me*: It was customary to save one of the best sheets to wrap the dead body before burial.
24   *you talk*: you're talking nonsense.
25   *Barbary*: an old form of 'Barbara'.

27   *of 'Willow'*: called 'Willow'; the willow-tree was the emblem of forsaken lovers. Desdemona's song intensifies the pathos of the scene.
30   *I have much to do*: I find it hard to stop myself.
32   *dispatch*: hurry up.

33   *night-gown*: dressing-gown.

34   *proper*: good-looking; the two women discuss the departed guest.

35   *speaks well*: talks interestingly.

37 *touch ... lip*: a kiss.

38 *sycamore*: probably a kind of fig-tree.

45 *Lay by these*: Put away these (i.e. her jewels).

47 *hie thee*: go away.

50 *that's not next*: The line that Desdemona has just sung does not come from the song—but it tells of her own feelings towards Othello.

54 *moe*: an obsolete (poetic) form of 'more'. *couch*: sleep.

56 *bode*: foretell.

58 *in conscience*: honestly.

60 *such gross kind*: i.e. by committing adultery.

to Palestine for a touch of his nether lip.
    Desdemona
[*Sings*]
    The poor soul sat sighing by a sycamore tree,
      Sing all a green willow;
40   Her hand on her bosom, her head on her knee,
      Sing willow, willow, willow;
    The fresh streams ran by her and murmured her
      moans;
      Sing willow, willow, willow;
    Her salt tears fell from her and softened the
      stones—
                    [*She speaks*]
45 Lay by these.
         [*She sings*]
    Sing willow, willow, willow—
         [*She speaks*]
Prithee hie thee; he'll come anon.
         [*She sings*]
    Sing all a green willow must be my garland.
    Let nobody blame him; his scorn I approve—
        [*She speaks*]
50 Nay, that's not next. Hark, who is't that knocks?
    Emilia
It's the wind.
    Desdemona
[*Sings*]
    I called my love false love, but what said he
      then?
      Sing willow, willow, willow:
    If I court moe women, you'll couch with moe
      men.
        [*She speaks*]
55 So get thee gone; good night. Mine eyes do itch:
Does that bode weeping?
    Emilia   'Tis neither here nor there.
    Desdemona
I have heard it said so. O, these men, these men!
Dost thou in conscience think—tell me, Emilia—
That there be women do abuse their husbands
60 In such gross kind?
    Emilia   There be some such, no question.
    Desdemona
Wouldst thou do such a deed for all the world?

62 *by this heavenly light*: perhaps Desdemona is swearing by God's light, although Emilia (in an attempt to amuse her mistress) assumes that the reference is to the moonlight.

67 *small vice*: Emilia dismisses the sin that is causing so much anguish to Othello and Desdemona.

69 *undo't*: cancel; probably Emilia means that she would deny the adultery.
70 *joint ring*: a ring made in two separate parts.
71 *measures of lawn*: lengths of fabric.
72 *exhibition*: allowance of money.
73 *'Ud's pity*: Emilia swears by 'God's pity', an oath that was omitted (probably for reasons of censorship) from the Folio text—see p.iv.
75 *venture purgatory*: risk being condemned to purgatory.

82 *to th'vantage*: in addition.
83 *store*: populate.
84 *But I do think*: This is the first time in the play that Emilia has been allowed to speak her real mind; Desdemona seems not to hear, being absorbed in her own troubled thoughts.
85 *fall*: sin.
     slack their duties: fail to perform their sexual obligations.
86 Making love to other women.
88 *Throwing ... us*: Restricting our freedom.
89 *scant*: reduce.
     former having: what we used to have.
     in despite: out of spite.
90 *galls*: spirits capable of resentment.
     grace: i.e. to forgive them.
92 *sense*: feelings.

Emilia
Why, would not you?
    Desdemona   No, by this heavenly light.
    Emilia
Nor I neither by this heavenly light: I might do't as well i'th dark.
    Desdemona
65 Wouldst thou do such a deed for all the world?
    Emilia
The world's a huge thing: it is a great price for a small vice.
    Desdemona
In troth, I think thou wouldst not.
    Emilia
In troth I think I should, and undo't when I had done
70 it. Marry, I would not do such a thing for a joint ring, nor for measures of lawn, nor for gowns, petticoats, nor caps, nor any petty exhibition. But for all the whole world! 'Ud's pity, who would not make her husband a cuckold, to make him a monarch? I should
75 venture purgatory for't.
    Desdemona
Beshrew me, if I would do such a wrong for the whole world!
    Emilia
Why, the wrong is but a wrong i'th'world; and having the world for your labour, 'tis wrong in your
80 own world, and you might quickly make it right.
    Desdemona
I do not think there is any such woman.
    Emilia
Yes, a dozen: and as many to th'vantage
as would store the world they played for.
But I do think it is their husband's faults
85 If wives do fall. Say that they slack their duties,
And pour our treasures into foreign laps;
Or else break out in peevish jealousies,
Throwing restraint upon us; or say they strike us,
Or scant our former having in despite—
90 Why, we have galls; and though we have some grace,
Yet have we some revenge. Let husbands know
Their wives have sense like them: they see and
    smell,

95   *sport*: for amusement.
96   *affection*: desire.
100 *use us well*: treat us kindly.
101 *ills*: wrongs.
     instruct us so: teach us to do the same.
102 *Good night*: Throughout Emilia's worldly-
     wise soliloquy, Desdemona has been silent;
     now she articulates a quite different
     philosophy.
103 *pick*: learn.
     by bad mend: amend myself by learning
     from bad examples, *or* from my own
     suffering.

And have their palates both for sweet and sour
As husbands have. What is it that they do,
95 When they change us for others? Is it sport?
I think it is. And doth affection breed it?
I think it doth. Is't frailty that thus errs?
It is so too. And have not we affections,
Desires for sport, and frailty, as men have?
100 Then let them use us well: else let them know
The ills we do, their ills instruct us so.
Desdemona
Good night, good night. God me such uses send,
Not to pick bad from bad, but by bad mend! [*Exeunt*

Act 5

Act 5   Scene 1

It is now late at night—'between twelve and one', as Iago promised Roderigo at the end of *Act 4, Scene 2*. The two men are close to Bianca's house, where they are lying in wait for Cassio. There is a scuffle in which both Cassio and Roderigo are wounded. Othello surveys the scene, misinterpreting—but approving—Iago's work; then he hurries off to Desdemona. Iago appears to investigate the disturbance and, fearing lest Roderigo should betray the plot, kills him. When Bianca tries to help, Iago accuses her of conspiracy; he then ensures that Cassio is carried to safety, and insists that Othello must be informed. After the peaceful sadness of the last scene in Desdemona's chamber, the action bursts into violence.

1 *bulk*: projecting wall— which on the stage would be represented by a pillar.
   straight: immediately.
2 *bare*: unsheathed.
   put it home: thrust it in deeply.
3 *at thy elbow*: near at hand, ready to help.
4 *makes ... us*: makes our fortunes, or else ruins us—a proverbial expression.
5 *resolution*: determination.
6 *miscarry*: make a mistake.
7 *take thy stand*: stand firm—don't run away; it is characteristic of Iago that he should make Roderigo strike the first blow.
8 *devotion in*: enthusiasm for.
11 *young quat*: little spot.
   sense: quick—where it hurts most.
14 *makes my gain*: I win.
   Live Roderigo: If Roderigo lives.

Scene 1

Enter Iago *and* Roderigo

Iago
Here, stand behind this bulk: straight will he come.
Wear thy good rapier bare, and put it home,
Quick, quick; fear nothing: I'll be at thy elbow.
It makes us, or it mars us; think on that,
5 And fix most firm thy resolution.
Roderigo
Be near at hand; I may miscarry in't.
Iago
Here, at thy hand: be bold, and take thy stand.
                                                      [*He retires*
Roderigo
I have no great devotion to the deed,
And yet he hath given me satisfying reasons.
10 'Tis but a man gone. Forth my sword! He dies!
Iago
I have rubbed this young quat almost to the sense,
And he grows angry. Now, whether he kill Cassio,
Or Cassio him, or each do kill the other,
Every way makes my gain. Live Roderigo,
15 He calls me to a restitution large
Of gold and jewels, that I bobbed from him
As gifts to Desdemona.
It must not be. If Cassio do remain
He hath a daily beauty in his life
20 That makes me ugly: and besides, the Moor
May unfold me to him—there stand I in much peril.
No, he must die. But soft, I hear him coming.

15 *calls me to*: demands from me.
    large: full.
16 *bobbed from him*: cheated him out of.
19 *daily beauty*: Iago recognizes in Cassio an
    admirable quality of life which is there for
    all to see.
21 *unfold*: expose.
22 *soft*: hush.
23 *gait*: footsteps.
25 *coat*: probably Cassio is wearing a leather
    jerkin.
26 *make proof of*: test.

27s.d. *above*: on the balcony behind the stage
    (see p6).

29 *even so*: Othello seems to mistake
    Roderigo's voice for Cassio's.

33 *Minion*: A term of abuse (or affection).
    dear: beloved.
34 *unblest fate*: cursed end.
    hies: is coming fast.
35 *blotted*: wiped out.
36 *lust-stained*: defiled with lust.
    lust's blood: the blood of your lustful body.

36s.d. *Gratiano*: He has just arrived from
    Venice with the news of Brabantio's death
    (see *Act 5, Scene 2, line 203*).
37 *watch*: night-watchman.
    passage: passers-by.

38 *mischance*: accident.
    direful: in great distress.

Enter Cassio

Roderigo
I know his gait; 'tis he. Villain, thou diest!
Cassio
That thrust had been mine enemy indeed,
25 But that my coat is better than thou think'st
I will make proof of thine.

He wounds Roderigo

Roderigo   O, I am slain!
            [Iago *wounds* Cassio *in the leg, and exits*
Cassio
I am maimed for ever. Help, ho! Murder, murder!

Enter Othello, *above*

Othello
The voice of Cassio: Iago keeps his word.
Roderigo
O villain that I am!
Othello   It is even so.
Cassio
30 O help, ho! Light! A surgeon!
Othello
'Tis he! O brave Iago, honest and just,
That hast such noble sense of thy friend's wrong,
Thou teachest me! Minion, your dear lies dead,
And your unblest fate hies. Strumpet, I come!
35 Forth of my heart those charms, thine eyes, are
        blotted;
Thy bed, lust-stained, shall with lust's blood be
        spotted.
                                [*Exit* Othello

Enter Lodovico *and* Gratiano

Cassio
What ho! No watch? No passage? Murder, murder!
Gratiano
'Tis some mischance: the cry is very direful.
Cassio
O help!
Lodovico
40 Hark!

42 *heavy*: dark.
43 *counterfeits*: impostors.
44 *in to the cry*: to the rescue; Lodovico and Gratiano are strangers in a foreign town, and their hesitation is understandable.

Roderigo
O wretched villain!

Lodovico
Two or three groan. It is a heavy night.
These may be counterfeits. Let's think't unsafe
To come in to the cry without more help.

Roderigo
45 Nobody come? Then shall I bleed to death.

Lodovico
Hark!

Enter Iago, *with a light*

47 *one*: someone; Iago appears as though he has been roused from his bed.

Gratiano
Here's one comes in his shirt, with light and
        weapons.

Iago
Who's there? Whose noise is this that cries on
        murder?

Lodovico
I do not know.

Iago   Did you not hear a cry?

Cassio
50 Here, here: for heaven's sake help me!

Iago   What's the matter?

Gratiano
This is Othello's ancient, as I take it.

Lodovico
The same indeed, a very valiant fellow.

Iago
What are you here, that cry so grievously?

54 *spoiled*: wounded.
   undone: injured.

Cassio
Iago? O I am spoiled, undone by villains!
55 Give me some help.

Iago
O me, lieutenant! What villains have done this?

Cassio
I think that one of them is hereabout
And cannot make away.

58 *make away*: escape.

Iago   O treacherous villains!
What are you there? Come in, and give some help.

Roderigo
60 O help me here!

Cassio

That's one of them.

Iago   O murd'rous slave! O villain!

He stabs Roderigo

Roderigo

O damned Iago! O inhuman dog!

He faints

Iago

Kill men i'th'dark? Where be these bloody thieves?
How silent is this town! Ho, murder, murder!

Lodovico *and* Gratiano *come forward*

65   What may you be? Are you of good or evil?

Lodovico

66   Judge us (to be good or evil) when you
know who we are.

As you shall prove us, praise us.

Iago

Signor Lodovico?

Lodovico

He, sir.

Iago

69   *cry you mercy*: beg your pardon.

I cry you mercy. Here's Cassio hurt by villains.

Gratiano

70   Cassio?

Iago

How is't, brother?

Cassio

My leg is cut in two.

Iago   Marry, heaven forbid!
Light, gentlemen. I'll bind it with my shirt.

Enter Bianca

Bianca

What is the matter, ho? Who is't that cried?

Iago

75   Who is't that cried?

Bianca

O my dear Cassio, my sweet Cassio,
O Cassio, Cassio, Cassio!

Iago

78   *may you suspect*: can you guess?
79   *mangled*: wounded.

O notable strumpet! Cassio, may you suspect
Who they should be that have thus mangled you?

Cassio

80 No.

Gratiano

I am sorry to find you thus: I have been to seek you.

Iago

Lend me a garter: so. O for a chair

To bear him easily hence!

Bianca   Alas, he faints!

O Cassio, Cassio, Cassio!

Iago

85 Gentlemen all, I do suspect this trash

To be a party in this injury.

Patience awhile, good Cassio. Come, come,

Lend me a light. Know we this face or no?

Alas, my friend, and my dear countryman

90 Roderigo? No—yes, sure—O heaven, Roderigo!

Gratiano

What! Of Venice?

Iago

Even he, sir. Did you know him?

Gratiano   Know him? Ay.

Iago

Signor Gratiano? I cry you gentle pardon.

These bloody accidents must excuse my manners

95 That so neglected you.

Gratiano   I am glad to see you.

Iago

How do you, Cassio? O a chair, a chair!

Gratiano

Roderigo!

Iago

He, he, 'tis he.

Enter Attendants *with chair*

O that's well said, the chair!

Some good man bear him carefully from hence.

100 I'll fetch the general's surgeon. For you, mistress,

Save you your labour. He that lies slain here, Cassio,

Was my dear friend. What malice was between you?

Cassio

None in the world, nor do I know the man.

82 *garter*: Either a man or a woman could supply this—to fix the bandage made with Iago's shirt.

85 *trash*: Iago insults Bianca.
86 *be a party*: have a share in.

98 *said*: done.

101 *Save you your labour*: Stop interfering.

Iago

[*to* Bianca] What, look you pale? O, bear him out
o'th'air.

    [Cassio *is borne in*. Roderigo's *body is removed*

105 Stay you, good gentlemen. Look you pale, mistress?

106   *gastness*: look of terror.

Do you perceive the gastness of her eye?
Nay, if you stare, we shall hear more anon.
Behold her well; I pray you look upon her.
Do you see, gentlemen? Nay, guiltiness will speak

110 Though tongues were out of use.

    Enter Emilia

Emilia

'Las, what's the matter? What's the matter, husband?

Iago

Cassio hath here been set on in the dark

113   *scaped*: escaped.

By Roderigo and fellows that are scaped:
He's almost slain and Roderigo quite dead.

Emilia

115 Alas, good gentleman! Alas, good Cassio!

Iago

This is the fruit of whoring. Prithee, Emilia,

117   *know of*: find out from.

Go know of Cassio where he supped tonight.
What, do you shake at that?

Bianca

119   *I therefore shake not*: I'm not afraid to say
    so.

He supped at my house, but I therefore shake not.

120   *charge*: order.

Iago

120 O did he so? I charge you go with me.

Emilia

O fie upon thee, strumpet!

Bianca

I am no strumpet, but of life as honest
As you that thus abuse me.

Emilia   As I? Foh! Fie upon thee!

Iago

124   *dressed*: have his wound attended to.

Kind gentlemen, let's see poor Cassio dressed.

125 Come, mistress, you must tell's another tale.
Emilia, run you to the citadel,

127   *happed*: chanced.

And tell my lord and lady what hath happed.
Will you go on afore? [*Aside*] This is the night

129   *fordoes*: ruins.
    quite: utterly.

That either makes me, or fordoes me quite.   [*Exeunt*

Act 5   Scene 2

Othello has hurried from the scene of the
fight and found Desdemona asleep in bed.
The sight of her beauty almost dissuades
him from his purpose, but when she wakes
he accuses her of adultery with Cassio and
declares his intentions. Despite Desdemona's
pleas, he kills her. Emilia discovers the
situation, but when Othello tells her his
reasons for the murder she is able to
proclaim Desdemona's innocence and
declare Iago's guilt in slandering her. Iago
arrives with the Venetian nobles, and all is
revealed. Othello is prevented from attacking
Iago, but Iago seizes an opportunity to kill
Emilia. The wounded Cassio is brought to
the scene and Othello, horrified at the
misjudgement he has made, asks Cassio's
pardon. Iago is condemned to torture and
Othello is arrested by Lodovico. But before
he is taken away, Othello has one last
speech to deliver and a final deed to
perform. This long last scene is beautifully
constructed, intermingling speeches of
powerful eloquence with simple
straightforward dialogue.

os.d.   *Desdemona in her bed*: Desdemona's bed
would probably be in the curtained recess
under the balcony (see p6); the bed
could be pushed forward on to the main
stage as the scene starts.

1   *It is the cause*: Othello believes that he is
killing Desdemona for a good
reason—sacrificing her to an ideal rather
than murdering in vengeful hatred.

2   *it*: the offence—i.e. adultery.

4   *whiter ... snow*: skin which is whiter than
snow.

5   *monumental alabaster*: Statues and figures on
tombs were often carved from alabaster,
which is a translucent white stone.

6   *betray*: cause them to commit adultery.

7   *the light*: i.e. the torch that he is carrying;
but the second 'light' in this line refers to
Desdemona's life.

8   *flaming minister*: the useful burning torch.

10   *Should ... me*: If I regret what I have done.

11   Othello sees Desdemona as the most
cleverly ('cunning'st') created product of all-
excelling nature.

12   *Promethean heat*: In some Greek legends,
Prometheus stole fire from the gods and
used it to animate the clay figures he had
made, thus creating the first human beings.

Scene 2

Enter Othello, *with a light,* Desdemona *in
her bed*

Othello
It is the cause, it is the cause, my soul:
Let me not name it to you, you chaste stars!
It is the cause. Yet I'll not shed her blood,
Nor scar that whiter skin of hers than snow,
5   And smooth as monumental alabaster:
Yet she must die, else she'll betray more men.
Put out the light, and then put out the light:
If I quench thee, thou flaming minister,
I can again thy former light restore,
10   Should I repent me; but once put out thy light,
Thou cunning'st pattern of excelling nature,
I know not where is that Promethean heat
That can thy light relume. When I have plucked the
    rose,
I cannot give it vital growth again,
15   It needs must wither. I'll smell it on the tree.

He kisses her

O balmy breath, that dost almost persuade
Justice to break her sword! One more, one more.
Be thus when thou art dead and I will kill thee,
And love thee after. One more, and this the last.
20 So sweet was ne'er so fatal. I must weep.
But they are cruel tears: this sorrow's heavenly—
It strikes where it doth love. She wakes!

Desdemona

Who's there? Othello?

    Othello

Ay, Desdemona.

    Desdemona   Will you come to bed, my lord?

    Othello

25 Have you prayed tonight, Desdemon?

    Desdemona   Ay, my lord.

    Othello

If you bethink yourself of any crime
Unreconciled as yet to heaven and grace,
Solicit for it straight.

    Desdemona

Alack, my lord, what may you mean by that?

    Othello

30 Well, do it, and be brief; I will walk by:
I would not kill thy unprepared spirit;
No—heaven forfend!—I would not kill thy soul.

    Desdemona

Talk you of killing?

    Othello   Ay, I do.

    Desdemona   Then heaven
Have mercy on me!

    Othello   Amen, with all my heart!

    Desdemona

35 If you say so, I hope you will not kill me.

    Othello

Hum!

    Desdemona

And yet I fear you: for you're fatal then
When your eyes roll so. Why I should fear I know
   not,
Since guiltiness I know not; but yet I feel I fear.

    Othello

40 Think on thy sins.

    Desdemona   They are loves I bear to you.

13 *relume*: re-kindle.
14 *vital growth*: life.
15 *needs must*: is forced to.
17 *Justice ... sword*: Othello sees himself as the agent (or even the personification) of Justice, who is traditionally depicted with a sword.
20 *So ... fatal*: Nothing was ever so sweet and so deadly.
21 *cruel tears*: Othello weeps because he loves Desdemona and because she has (as he thinks) betrayed their love; if he had no cause for tears, he would have no cause to kill her.
21-2 *heavenly ... love*: has a divine nature because it punishes the one it loves, like the God described in the Epistle to the Hebrews: 'whom the Lord loveth, he chasteneth' (12:6).
26 *bethink yourself*: remember.
27 Othello refers to the Christian teaching about the confession and forgiveness of sin.
28 *Solicit*: Pray pardon.
   straight: now.
30 *by*: aside; he will allow privacy for her confession.
31 *unprepared spirit*: i.e. not prepared for death (by making a full confession).
32 *forfend*: forbid.
   kill thy soul: Othello accepts the orthodox Catholic teaching that those who die without confessing their sins will be damned.
37 *fatal*: terrible.
38 *your eyes roll so*: An indication how the part should be played, or was being played. This would be a useful guide on the Jacobean stage; see also line 43.
40 *loves*: Desdemona is perhaps thinking of the disobedience to her father.

42 It is unnatural to kill someone for loving.
43 *nether*: bottom.
44 *very frame*: whole body.
45 *portènts*: bad signs.
46 *do not point on*: are not directed at.

47 *will—so*: Desdemona controls herself in the space between these two words.

52 *presently*: at once.
53 *freely*: fully.
54 *article*: item of which she is accused.
55 *choke*: kill by strangling.
    conception: suspicion; the imagery is confirmed in the next line.
56 *groan withal*: labour with; Othello's suspicions of Desdemona are causing pain like birth pangs.

60 *general warranty*: ordinary permission.

63 *stone my heart*: turn my heart to stone.
64-5 Desdemona's refusal to confess her guilt makes her unfit to be a sacrificial victim, and Othello must now consider himself a murderer.

67 *Send ... hither*: Order him to come here.

Othello
Ay, and for that thou diest.
Desdemona
That death's unnatural that kills for loving.
Alas, why gnaw you so your nether lip?
Some bloody passion shakes your very frame:
45 These are portènts; but yet I hope, I hope
They do not point on me.
Othello   Peace, and be still!
Desdemona
I will—so. What's the matter?
Othello
That handkerchief which I so loved and gave thee,
Thou gav'st to Cassio.
Desdemona   No, by my life and soul!
50 Send for the man and ask him.
Othello   Sweet soul, take heed,
Take heed of perjury: thou art on thy death-bed.
Desdemona
Ay, but not yet to die.
Othello   Yes, presently.
Therefore confess thee freely of thy sin;
For to deny each article with oath
55 Cannot remove nor choke the strong conception
That I do groan withal. Thou art to die.
Desdemona
Then Lord have mercy on me!
Othello   I say, amen.
Desdemona
And have you mercy too! I never did
Offend you in my life; never loved Cassio
60 But with such general warranty of heaven
As I might love. I never gave him token.
Othello
By heaven, I saw my handkerchief in's hand!
O perjured woman! Thou dost stone my heart,
And mak'st me call what I intend to do
65 A murder, which I thought a sacrifice.
I saw the handkerchief.
Desdemona   He found it then.
I never gave it him. Send for him hither.
Let him confess a truth.
Othello   He hath confessed.

Desdemona
What, my lord?
Othello

70 That he hath used thee.

70 *used thee*: had some relationship with you.

    Desdemona   How? Unlawfully?
Othello
Ay.
Desdemona
He will not say so.
    Othello   No, his mouth is stopped:
Honest Iago hath ta'en order for't.

72 *his mouth is stopped*: he has been silenced.
73 *ta'en order for't*: seen to it.

Desdemona
O my fear interprets! What, is he dead?
Othello

74 *my fear interprets*: I am afraid I understand.

75 Had all his hairs been lives, my great revenge
Had stomach for them all.

75 *Had ... lives*: If he had had as many lives as the hairs on his head.
76 *stomach*: appetite.

Desdemona
Alas, he is betrayed, and I undone.
Othello
Out, strumpet! Weep'st thou for him to my face?

77 *undone*: ruined. Desdemona means that if Cassio is dead, he will not be able to vouch for her innocence; but Othello takes 'undone' to be an admission of guilt.

Desdemona
O banish me, my lord, but kill me not!
Othello

80 Down, strumpet!
Desdemona
Kill me tomorrow: let me live tonight!
Othello
Nay, if you strive—
Desdemona
But half an hour!
    Othello   Being done, there is no pause.

83 *Being ... pause*: Now that I have started, I must go on.

84 *But*: Just.

Desdemona
But while I say one prayer!
    Othello   It is too late.
Desdemona

85 O Lord, Lord, Lord!

He smothers her

Emilia
[*Without*] My lord, my lord! What ho! My lord, my lord!
Othello
What noise is this? Not dead? Not yet quite dead?

88-9   Othello is cruel enough to murder
Desdemona, but merciful enough to want to
ease the pain.

I, that am cruel, am yet merciful:
I would not have thee linger in thy pain.
90 So, so.

    Emilia [*Without*] What ho! My lord, my lord!
    Othello   Who's there?
    Emilia
[*Without*] O good my lord, I'd speak a word with
  you.
    Othello
Yes, 'tis Emilia.—By and by.—She's dead.

93   *like*: likely.
94   *high*: loud.

'Tis like she comes to speak of Cassio's death:
The noise was high. Ha! No more moving?
95 Still as the grave. Shall she come in? Were't good?
I think she stirs again. No. What's best to do?
If she come in, she'll sure speak to my wife—
My wife! My wife! What wife? I have no wife.
O insupportable! O heavy hour!

99   *insupportable*: I can't bear it; Othello has
begun to regret his deed.

101 *globe*: the whole world.
102 *yawn*: tear itself apart (in an earthquake).
Othello is looking for the sort of confusion
that might be associated with the end of the
world.
 alteration: the change brought about by
Desdemona's death.

100 Methinks it should be now a huge eclipse
Of sun and moon, and that th'affrighted globe
Should yawn at alteration.
    Emilia   I do beseech you
That I may speak with you. O good my lord!
    Othello
I had forgot thee. O come in, Emilia.
105 Soft; by and by. Let me the curtains draw.
Where art thou? [*He unlocks the door.*] What's the
  matter with thee now?

       Enter Emilia

    Emilia
O my good lord, yonder's foul murder done.
    Othello
What! Now?
    Emilia
But now, my lord.
    Othello

110-12 It was believed that the influence of
the moon could make people insane.
 error: wandering.
 was wont: used to do.

110 It is the very error of the moon;
She comes more nearer earth than she was wont,
And makes men mad.
    Emilia
Cassio, my lord, hath killed a young Venetian
Called Roderigo.
    Othello   Roderigo killed?

115 And Cassio killed?

Emilia   No, Cassio is not killed.

Othello

116 *out of tune*: gone wrong.

Not Cassio killed! Then murder's out of tune,
And sweet revenge grows harsh.

Desdemona

118 Desdemona revives for a moment.

O falsely, falsely murdered!

Emilia   O Lord! What cry is that?

Othello

That? What?

Emilia

120 Out and alas, that was my lady's voice!

She draws back the curtains

Help, help, ho, help! O lady, speak again!
Sweet Desdemona, O sweet mistress, speak!

Desdemona

A guiltless death I die.

Emilia

O who hath done this deed?

Desdemona

125 Nobody—I myself—farewell.
Commend me to my kind lord—O farewell!   [*She dies*

Othello

Why, how should she be murdered?

Emilia   Alas, who knows?

Othello

You heard her say herself it was not I.

Emilia

She said so: I must needs report the truth.

Othello

130 *like a liar*: like the liar that she is.

130 She's like a liar gone to burning hell:
'Twas I that killed her.

Emilia   O the more angel she,
And you the blacker devil!

Othello

133 *folly*: sin.

She turned to folly; and she was a whore.

Emilia

Thou dost belie her, and thou art a devil.

Othello

135 She was false as water.

Emilia   Thou art rash as fire to say
That she was false. O, she was heavenly true!

137   *top*: Othello picks up Iago's word
       (3,3,393).
          else: if it's not true.
139   *But*: Except.
140   *extremity*: final act.

144   *entire*: pure.
          chrysolite: topaz (a semi-precious stone);
       but I think that the word may have been
       chosen not for its meaning but because of
       its sound.

149   *iterance*: repetition.

150   *made mocks with*: made a fool of.

155   *half a grain a day*: very, very slowly.
          lies to th'heart: completely.
156   *too fond of*: infatuated with.
          most filthy bargain: i.e. the husband for
       whom she paid such a high price.

159   *no more worthy heaven*: presumably Emilia
       means that the deed is damnable.
160   *Peace ... best*: You had better shut up.
161-2 I can endure far more than you are able
       to inflict upon me.

162   *gull*: fool.
          dolt: idiot.

Othello
Cassio did top her: ask thy husband else.
O, I were damned beneath all depth in hell
But that I did proceed upon just grounds
140   To this extremity. Thy husband knew it all.
          Emilia
My husband!
          Othello   Thy husband.
          Emilia   That she was false to wedlock?
          Othello
Ay, with Cassio. Nay, had she been true,
If heaven would make me such another world
Of one entire and perfect chrysolite,
145   I'd not have sold her for it.
          Emilia   My husband!
          Othello
Ay, 'twas he that told me on her first.
An honest man he is, and hates the slime
That sticks on filthy deeds.
          Emilia   My husband!
          Othello
What needs this iterance, woman? I say thy husband.
          Emilia
150   O mistress, villainy hath made mocks with love!
My husband say that she was false?
          Othello   He, woman;
I say thy husband; dost understand the word?
My friend, thy husband, honest, honest, Iago.
          Emilia
If he say so, may his pernicious soul
155   Rot half a grain a day! He lies to th'heart.
She was too fond of her most filthy bargain.
          Othello
Ha!
          Emilia
Do thy worst:
This deed of thine is no more worthy heaven
160   Than thou wast worthy her.
          Othello   Peace, you were best.
          Emilia
Thou hast not half the power to do me harm
As I have to be hurt. O gull! O dolt!
As ignorant as dirt! Thou hast done a deed—

164 *I care ... sword*: i.e. don't threaten me.

I care not for thy sword—I'll make thee known,
165 Though I lost twenty lives. Help! Help, ho! Help!
The Moor hath killed my mistress! Murder! Murder!

Enter Montano, Gratiano, *and* Iago

Montano
What is the matter? How now, general?
Emilia
O, are you come, Iago? You have done well,

169 *lay ... neck*: blame you for their murders.

That men must lay their murders on your neck.
Gratiano
170 What is the matter?
Emilia
Disprove this villain, if thou be'st a man:
He says thou told'st him that his wife was false.
I know thou didst not: thou'rt not such a villain.
Speak, for my heart is full.
Iago
175 I told him what I thought, and told no more

176 *apt*: reasonable.

Than what he found himself was apt and true.
Emilia
But did you ever tell him she was false?
Iago
I did.
Emilia
You told a lie, an odious damnèd lie:
180 Upon my soul, a lie, a wicked lie!
She false with Cassio! Did you say with Cassio?
Iago

182 *charm*: hold.

With Cassio, mistress! Go to, charm your tongue.
Emilia
I will not charm my tongue; I am bound to speak:
My mistress here lies murdered in her bed.
All
185 O heavens forfend!
Emilia

186 *set ... on*: caused the murder.

And your reports have set the murder on.
Othello
Nay, stare not, masters: it is true indeed.
Gratiano
'Tis a strange truth.
Montano
O monstrous act!

Emilia   Villainy, villainy, villainy!
190 I think upon't, I think—I smell't—O villainy!
I thought so then; I'll kill myself for grief.
O villainy, villainy!
Iago
What, are you mad? I charge you get you home.
Emilia
Good gentlemen, let me have leave to speak.
195 'Tis proper I obey him, but not now.
Perchance, Iago, I will ne'er go home.
Othello
[*Falling on bed*] O! O! O!
Emilia   Nay, lay thee down and roar,
For thou hast killed the sweetest innocent
That e'er did lift up eye.
Othello [*rising*]   O, she was foul!
200 I scarce did know you, uncle; there lies your niece,
Whose breath indeed these hands have newly
    stopped.
I know this act shows horrible and grim.
Gratiano
Poor Desdemon, I am glad thy father's dead:
Thy match was mortal to him, and pure grief
205 Shore his old thread in twain. Did he live now,
This sight would make him do a desperate turn,
Yea, curse his better angel from his side,
And fall to reprobance.
Othello
'Tis pitiful: but yet Iago knows
210 That she with Cassio hath the act of shame
A thousand times committed. Cassio confessed it,
And she did gratify his amorous works
With that recognizance and pledge of love
Which I first gave her. I saw it in his hand:
215 It was a handkerchief, an antique token
My father gave my mother.
Emilia   O God! O heavenly God!
Iago
Zounds, hold your peace!
Emilia   'Twill out, 'twill out. I peace?
No, I will speak as liberal as the north;
Let heaven, and men, and devils, let them all,

195 Emilia acknowledges the ruling that a wife should obey her husband, but she will not obey Iago now.
197 *roar*: howl.

200 *scarce did know you, uncle*: hardly recognized you; Othello speaks to Gratiano, Desdemona's uncle and therefore (by marriage) his own.

204 *match*: marriage.
    mortal: fatal.
205 *Shore ... twain*: Cut the thread of his life in two.
    Did he live now: If he were alive now.
206 *turn*: deed.
207 He would drive away his guardian angel.
208 *reprobance*: a state of damnation.
210 *the act of shame*: adultery.
211 *a thousand times*: the expression is purely rhetorical, intended for emphasis not accuracy.
212 *gratify*: reward.
    amorous works: love-making.
213 *recognizance*: token.
215 *antique*: ancient.
216 Shakespeare seems to have forgotten that in *Act 3*, Scene 4 Othello told Desdemona that the handkerchief was given to his mother by an Egyptian (lines 51-5).
    O heavenly God: In the Folio text Emilia calls on the 'heavenly Powers'.
217 *'Twill out*: It [the truth] must come out.
    I peace: Must I keep quiet.
218 *liberal as the north*: as unrestrained as the north wind—a particularly violent and bitterly cold wind.

220 All, all cry shame against me, yet I'll speak.
        Iago
Be wise, and get you home.
        Emilia   I will not.

Iago *draws his sword*

        Gratiano   Fie!
Your sword upon a woman!
        Emilia
O thou dull Moor, that handkerchief thou speak'st of
I found by fortune and did give my husband;
225 For often, with a solemn earnestness—
More than indeed belonged to such a trifle—
He begged of me to steal it.
        Iago   Villainous whore!
        Emilia
She give it Cassio? No, alas I found it,
And I did give't my husband.
        Iago   Filth, thou liest!
        Emilia
230 By heaven I do not, I do not, gentlemen.
O murderous coxcomb, what should such a fool
Do with so good a wife?
        Othello   Are there no stones in heaven
But what serve for the thunder? Precious villain!
        [*He runs at* Iago; Montano *disarms him;*
        Iago *stabs* Emilia *from behind and exits*
        Gratiano
The woman falls: sure he hath killed his wife.
        Emilia
235 Ay, ay: O lay me by my mistress' side.
        Gratiano
He's gone, but his wife's killed.
        Montano
'Tis a notorious villain. Take you this weapon,
Which I have here recovered from the Moor.
Come guard the door without: let him not pass,
240 But kill him rather. I'll after that same villain,
For 'tis a damnèd slave.
        [*Exeunt* Montano *and* Gratiano
        Othello   I am not valiant neither,
But every puny whipster gets my sword.

---

224 *by fortune*: by chance.

231 *coxcomb*: idiot.
232-3 *Are there ... thunder*: Are the only
    thunderbolts in heaven used for making
    thunder (and not for striking villains)?
233 *Precious*: A term used to intensify abuse.

237 *notorious*: absolute.
238 *recovered from*: taken away from.
239 *without*: from the outside.
    pass: get away.

241 *I ... neither*: Othello has lost the courage
    even to attack Iago.
242 Any poor little man can take away my
    sword; but Montano, surely, does not
    deserve the term 'whipster'.

243 *honour outlive honesty*: reputation last any longer than desert.
244 *bode*: foretell.
245-6 *play the swan ... music*: Emilia will imitate the swan, a bird which was believed to sing only once in its lifetime—just before it dies; the snatch of song unites Emilia with her mistress.
248 *So ... bliss*: May my soul be saved.

251 *a sword of Spain*: Toledo, in southern Spain, was famous for the manufacture of swords.
  the ice-brook's temper: the steel was 'tempered' (= given its toughness) by being plunged into an icy stream.
254 *suffer*: get hurt.

256 *naked*: unarmed.

258 *sustain*: support.

262 *stop*: arrest.

264 *weaponed*: armed.
265 *Here*: Othello means to kill himself.
  butt: goal.
266 *sea-mark*: beacon.
  utmost sail: last voyage.
267 *'Tis a lost fear*: There's nothing to be afraid of.
268 *Man*: Aim.
  rush: reed.

270 *ill-starred*: ill-fated.
271 *smock*: a woman's under-garment.
  at compt: on the Day of Judgement.

274 *thy chastity*: Othello finally admits the truth.

But why should honour outlive honesty?
Let it go all.
  Emilia What did thy song bode, lady?
245 Hark, canst thou hear me? I will play the swan
And die in music. [*Singing*] 'Willow, willow, willow.'
Moor, she was chaste; she loved thee, cruel Moor,
So come my soul to bliss, as I speak true;
So speaking as I think, I die, I die.   [*She dies*
  Othello
250 I have another weapon in this chamber:
It was a sword of Spain, the ice-brook's temper.
O here it is. Uncle, I must come forth.
  Gratiano
[*Within*] If thou attempt it, it will cost thee dear;
Thou hast no weapon, and perforce must suffer.
  Othello
255 Look in upon me then, and speak with me,
Or naked as I am I will assault thee.

          Enter Gratiano

  Gratiano
What is the matter?
  Othello   Behold, I have a weapon:
A better never did itself sustain
Upon a soldier's thigh. I have seen the day
260 That with this little arm and this good sword,
I have made my way through more impediments
Than twenty times your stop. But, O vain boast!—
Who can control his fate?—'Tis not so now.
Be not afraid, though you do see me weaponed:
265 Here is my journey's end, here is my butt
And very sea-mark of my utmost sail.
Do you go back dismayed? 'Tis a lost fear:
Man but a rush against Othello's breast,
And he retires. Where should Othello go?

          He goes to the bed

270 Now, how dost thou look now? O ill-starred wench
Pale as thy smock! When we shall meet at compt
This look of thine will hurl my soul from heaven
And fiends will snatch at it. Cold, cold, my girl,
Even like thy chastity.

275 *slave*: Othello means himself.
275–8 Othello now images to himself some of the medieval portrayals of hell.

278 *steep-down*: precipitous.

283 *fable*: i.e. that a devil has cloven feet.

287 *in my sense*: as I feel now.

289 *practice*: trap.

291 Othello speaks with bitter irony.

275 O cursèd, cursèd slave! Whip me, ye devils,
From the possession of this heavenly sight!
Blow me about in winds! Roast me in sulphur!
Wash me in steep-down gulfs of liquid fire!
O Desdemon! Dead Desdemon! Dead! O! O!

Enter Lodovico, Cassio *in a chair,*
Montano *and* Iago *with* Officers
Lodovico
280 Where is this rash and most unfortunate man?
Othello
That's he that was Othello: here I am.
Lodovico
Where is that viper? Bring the villain forth.
Othello
I look down towards his feet: but that's a fable.
If that thou be'st a devil, I cannot kill thee.

He wounds Iago

Lodovico
285 Wrench his sword from him.
Iago   I bleed, sir, but not killed.
Othello
I am not sorry neither; I'd have thee live,
For in my sense 'tis happiness to die.
Lodovico
O thou Othello, that wast once so good,
Fallen in the practice of a damnèd slave,
290 What shall be said to thee?
Othello   Why, anything:
An honourable murderer, if you will:
For naught did I in hate, but all in honour.
Lodovico
This wretch hath part confessed his villainy.
Did you and he consent in Cassio's death?
Othello
295 Ay.
Cassio
Dear general, I never gave you cause.
Othello
I do believe it, and I ask your pardon.
Will you, I pray, demand that demi-devil
Why he hath thus ensnared my soul and body?

Iago

300 Demand me nothing; what you know, you know:
From this time forth I never will speak word.

Lodovico

What! Not to pray!

Gratiano

Torments will ope your lips.

Othello   Well, thou dost best.

Lodovico

Sir, you shall understand what hath befallen,

305 Which, as I think, you know not. Here is a letter
Found in the pocket of the slain Roderigo,
And here another: the one of them imports
The death of Cassio, to be undertook
By Roderigo.

Othello   O villain!

Cassio   Most heathenish and most gross!

Lodovico

310 Now here's another discontented paper
Found in his pocket too; and this, it seems
Roderigo meant to have sent this damnèd villain,
But that, belike, Iago, in the nick,
Came in and satisfied him.

Othello   O the pernicious caitiff!

315 How came you, Cassio, by that handkerchief
That was my wife's?

Cassio   I found it in my chamber;
And he himself confessed but even now
That there he dropped it for a special purpose
Which wrought to his desire.

Othello   O fool, fool, fool!

Cassio

320 There is besides, in Roderigo's letter,
How he upbraids Iago, that he made him
Brave me upon the watch, whereon it came
That I was cast; and even but now he spake
After long seeming dead—Iago hurt him,

325 Iago set him on.

Lodovico

You must forsake this room and go with us.
Your power and your command is taken off
And Cassio rules in Cyprus. For this slave,
If there be any cunning cruelty

303 *Torments*: Torture.
thou dost best: you know best.

307 *imports*: concerns.

310 *discontented paper*: letter expressing dissatisfaction.

313 *belike*: probably.
in the nick: just in time.
314 *satisfied him*: stopped his complaints (by killing him).
315 *came you ... by*: did you acquire?

317 *but even now*: only just now.

319 *wrought to*: suited.

321 *upbraids*: reproaches.
322 *Brave*: Challenge.
on the watch: when I was on guard.
whereon it came: as a result of which.
323 *cast*: dismissed,
he: i.e. Roderigo.
325 *set him on*: incited him.
326 *forsake*: leave.

330 *hold him long*: make him suffer for a long
time.
331 *close*: confined.

334 *Soft you*: Wait a minute.

337 *unlucky*: unfortunate.
338 *nothing extenuate*: do not make excuses.
339 *set down*: write.
340 *wisely*: i.e. moderately.
341 *wrought*: provoked.
342 *Perplexed in the extreme*: Completely
bewildered.
343 *base Indian*: The American Indians were
well-known for their ignorance about the
value of precious stones; the Folio text has
'Judean', which some editors take to be a
reference to Judas Iscariot, who betrayed
Christ. I suspect, however, that if there is
any biblical allusion at all in this line, it is
to the 'pearl of great price' described in St
Matthew's Gospel (13:46), which is a
metaphor for heavenly bliss.
344 *sùbdued*: overcome (by grief).
345 *melting mood*: weeping.
347 *gum*: myrrh, which oozes from the trees
and is used in religious ceremonies of
sacrifice and atonement — which makes it
medicinable.
350 *traduced*: insulted.
351 *circumcisèd*: i.e. Muhammedan.
353 *period*: conclusion.

357 *Spartan dog*: Lodovico turns to Iago; the
hounds of Sparta were notoriously savage.
358 *fell*: cruel.
359 *loading*: burden.

361 *Let it be hid*: The bed would now be
drawn back into the recess under the
balcony, and the curtains drawn.

330 That can torment him much, and hold him long,
It shall be his. You shall close prisoner rest,
Till that the nature of your fault be known
To the Venetian state. Come, bring him away.

Othello
Soft you; a word or two before you go.
335 I have done the state some service and they know't:
No more of that. I pray you in your letters
When you shall these unlucky deeds relate
Speak of me as I am: nothing extenuate,
Nor set down aught in malice. Then must you speak
340 Of one that loved not wisely, but too well;
Of one, not easily jealous but, being wrought,
Perplexed in the extreme; of one whose hand
Like the base Indian threw a pearl away
Richer than all his tribe; of one whose sùbdued eyes,
345 Albeit unusèd to the melting mood,
Drop tears as fast as the Arabian trees
Their med'cinable gum. Set you down this:
And say, besides, that in Aleppo once
Where a malignant and a turbaned Turk
350 Beat a Venetian and traduced the state,
I took by th'throat the circumcisèd dog
And smote him thus.

He stabs himself

Lodovico
O bloody period!
Gratiano   All that's spoke is marred!
Othello
I kissed thee, ere I killed thee: no way but this,
355 Killing myself, to die upon a kiss.
[*He falls on the bed and dies*
Cassio
This did I fear, but thought he had no weapon,
For he was great of heart.
Lodovico   O, Spartan dog,
More fell than anguish, hunger, or the sea,
Look on the tragic loading of this bed:
360 This is thy work. The object poisons sight:
Let it be hid.

The curtains are drawn

361 *keep*: stay in.

363 *succeed*: legally descend.
364 *censure*: sentencing.

366-7 The slow formality of the rhymed
       couplet with its sighing alliteration brings
       the play to a solemn conclusion.

Gratiano, keep the house
And seize upon the fortunes of the Moor,
For they succeed on you. To you, lord governor,
Remains the censure of this hellish villain:
365 The time, the place, the torture, O, enforce it!
Myself will straight abroad, and to the state
This heavy act with heavy heart relate.   [*Exeunt*

The 'Willow' song

(Act 4, 3, 38)

1. The poor soul sat sigh - ing by a sy - ca - more tree, Sing all a green wil - low; Her hand on her bo - som, her head on her knee, Sing wil - low, wil - low, wil - low, wil - low; sing wil - low, wil - low, wil - low, wil - low must be my gar - land. Sing all a green wil - low; wil - low, wil-low, wil - low, sing all a green wil - low must be my gar - land.

2. The fresh streams ran by her and mur - mured her moans; Her salt tears fell from her and sof - tened the stones,

3. I called my love false love, but what said he then? If I court moe wo - men, you'll couch with moe men.

The Source of *Othello*

This passage is taken from *Gli Hecatommithi* by Giovanni Battista Cinthio translated by Geoffrey Bullough (*Narrative and Dramatic Sources of Shakespeare*, Vol.VII, 1973).

There was once in Venice a Moor, a very gallant man, who, because he was personally valiant and had given proof in warfare of great prudence and skilful energy, was very dear to the Signoria, who in rewarding virtuous actions ever advanced the interests of the Republic. It happened that a virtuous Lady of wondrous beauty called Disdemona, impelled not by female appetite but by the Moor's good qualities, fell in love with him, and he, vanquished by the Lady's beauty and noble mind, likewise was enamoured of her. So propitious was their mutual love that, although the Lady's relatives did all they could to make her take another husband, they were united in marriage and lived together in such concord and tranquillity while they remained in Venice, that never a word passed between them that was not loving.

It happened that the Venetian lords made a change in the forces that they used to maintain in Cyprus; and they chose the Moor as Commandant of the soldiers whom they sent there. Although he was pleased by the honour offered him ... yet his happiness was lessened when he considered the length and dangers of the voyage, thinking that Disdemona would be much troubled by it. The Lady, who had no other happiness on earth but the Moor ... could hardly wait for the hour when he would set off with his men, and she would accompany him to that honourable post ... Shortly afterwards, having donned his armour and made all ready for the journey, he embarked in the galley with his lady, and with a sea of the utmost tranquillity arrived safely in Cyprus.

The Moor had in his company an Ensign of handsome presence but the most scoundrelly nature in the world. He was in high favour with the Moor, who had no suspicion of his wickedness; for although he had the basest of minds, he so cloaked the vileness hidden in his heart with high sounding and noble words, and by his manner, that he showed himself in the likeness of a Hector or an Achilles. This false man had likewise taken to Cyprus his wife, a fair and honest young woman. Being an Italian she was much loved by the Moor's wife, and spent the greater part of the day with her.

In the same company there was also a Corporal who was very dear to the Moor. This man went frequently to the Moor's house and often dined with him and his wife. The Lady, knowing him so well liked by her husband, gave him proofs of the greatest kindness, and this was much appreciated by the Moor.

The wicked Ensign, taking no account of the faith he had pledged to his wife, and of the friendship, loyalty and obligations he owed the Moor, fell ardently in love with Disdemona ... He sought therefore in various ways, as deviously as he could, to make the Lady aware that he desired her. But she, whose every thought was for the Moor, never gave a thought to the Ensign ... And all the things he did to arouse her feelings for him had no more effect than if he had not tried them. Whereupon he imagined that this was because she was in love with the Corporal, and he wondered how he might remove the latter from her sight. Not only did he turn his mind to this, but the love which he had felt for the Lady now changed to the bitterest hate, and he gave himself up to studying how to bring it about that, once the Corporal were killed, if he himself could not enjoy the Lady, then the Moor should not have her either. Turning over in his mind divers schemes, all wicked and treacherous, in the end he decided to accuse her of adultery, and to make her husband believe that the Corporal was the adulterer ... Wherefore he set himself to wait until time and place opened a way for him to start his wicked enterprise.

Not long afterwards the Moor deprived the Corporal of his rank for having drawn his sword and wounded a soldier while on guard-duty. Disdemona was grieved by this and tried many times to reconcile the Moor with him. Whereupon the Moor told the rascally Ensign that his wife importuned him so much for the Corporal that he feared he would be obliged to reinstate him. The evil man saw in this a hint for setting in train the deceits he had planned, and said: 'Perhaps Disdemona has good cause to look on him so favourably!' 'Why is that?' asked the Moor. 'I do not wish,' said the Ensign, 'to come between man and wife, but if you keep your eyes open you will see for yourself.' Nor for all the Moor's inquiries would the Ensign go beyond this: nonetheless his words left such a sharp thorn in the Moor's mind, that he gave himself up to pondering intensely what they could mean. He became quite melancholy, and one day, when his wife was trying to soften his anger towards the Corporal, begging him not to condemn to oblivion the loyal service and friendship of many years just for one small fault, especially since the Corporal had been reconciled to the man he had struck, the Moor burst out in anger and said to her 'there must be a very powerful reason why you take such trouble for this fellow, for he is not your brother, nor even a kinsman, yet you have him so much at heart.'

The Lady, all courtesy and modesty, replied: 'I should not like you to be angry with me ... Only a very good purpose made me speak to you about this, but rather than have you angry with me I shall never say another word on the subject.'

The Moor, however, seeing the earnestness with which his wife had again pleaded for the Corporal, guessed that the Ensign's words had been intended to suggest that Disdemona was in love with the Corporal, and he went in deep depression to the scoundrel and urged him to speak more openly. The Ensign, intent on injuring the unfortunate Lady, after pretending not to wish to say anything that might displease the Moor, appeared to be overcome by his entreaties and said: 'I must confess that it grieves me greatly to have to tell you something that must be in the highest degree painful to you; but since you wish me to tell you, and the regard that I must have of your honour as my master spurs me on, I shall not fail in my duty to answer your request. You must know therefore that it is hard for your Lady to see the Corporal in disgrace for the simple reason that she takes her pleasure with him whenever he comes to your house. The woman has come to dislike your blackness.'

These words struck the Moor's heart to its core; but in order to learn more (although he believed what the Ensign had said to be true, through the suspicion already sown in his mind) he said, with a fierce look: 'I do not know what holds me back from cutting out that outrageous tongue of yours which has dared to speak such insults against my Lady!' Then the Ensign: 'Captain,' he said, 'I did not expect any other reward for my loving service; but since my duty and my care for your honour have carried me so far, I repeat that the matter stands exactly as you have just heard it, and if your Lady with a false show of love for you, has so blinded your eyes that you have not seen what you ought to have seen, that does not mean that I am not speaking the truth. For this Corporal has told me all, like one whose happiness does not seem complete until he has made someone else acquainted with it.' And he added: 'If I had not feared your wrath, I should, when he told me, have given him the punishment he deserved by killing him. But since letting you know what concerns you more than anyone else brings me so undeserved a reward, I wish that I had kept silent, for by doing so I should not have fallen into your displeasure.'

Then the Moor, in the utmost anguish, said, 'If you do not make me see with my own eyes what you have told me, be assured, I shall make you realize that it would have been better for you had you been born dumb.'

[For some time the Ensign wondered what to do next, because 'his knowledge of the Lady's chastity' made it seem impossible that he should ever be able to make the Moor believe him; and then, 'his thoughts twisting and turning in all directions, the scoundrel thought of a new piece of mischief.']

The Moor's wife often went ... to the house of the Ensign's wife, and stayed with her a good part of the day; wherefore seeing that she sometimes carried with her a handkerchief embroidered most delicately in the Moorish fashion, which the Moor had given her and which was treasured by the Lady and her husband too, the Ensign planned to take it from her secretly, and thereby prepare her final ruin. [One day, whilst Disdemona was playing with his child, the Ensign stole the handkerchief; he dropped it in the Corporal's room.]

[The Ensign] spoke to the Corporal one day while the Moor was standing where he could see them as they talked; and chatting of quite other matters than the Lady, he laughed heartily and, displaying great surprise, he moved his head about and gestured with his hands, acting as if he were listening to marvels. As soon as the Moor saw them separate he went to the Ensign to learn what the other had told him; and the Ensign, after making him entreat for a long time, finally declared: 'He has hidden nothing from me. He tells me that he has enjoyed your wife every time you have given them the chance by your absence, and on the last occasion she gave him the handkerchief which you gave her as a present when you married her.' The Moor thanked the Ensign and it seemed obvious to him that if he found that the Lady no longer had the handkerchief, then all must be as the Ensign claimed.

Wherefore one day after dinner ... he asked her for this handkerchief. The unhappy woman, who had greatly feared this, grew red in the face at the request ... 'I do not know,' she said, 'why I cannot find it.' ...

Leaving her, the Moor began to think how he might kill his wife, and the Corporal too, in such a way that he would not be blamed for it. And since he was obsessed with this, day and night, the Lady inevitably noticed that he was not the same towards her as he was formerly. Many times she said to him, 'What is the matter with you? What is troubling you? Whereas you used to be the gayest of men, you are now the most melancholy man alive.'

The Moor invented various excuses, but she was not at all satisfied ... Sometimes she would say to the Ensign's wife, 'I do not know what to make of the Moor. He used to be all love towards me, but in the last few days he has become quite another man; and I fear greatly that I shall be a warning to young girls not to marry against their parents' wishes; and Italian ladies will learn by my example not to tie themselves to a man whom Nature, Heaven, and the manner of life separate from us. But because I know that he is very friendly with your husband, and confides in him, I beg you, if you have learned anything from him which you can tell me, that you will not fail to help me.' She wept bitterly as she spoke...

The Corporal [who had recognized the handkerchief and tried, without success, to return it] had a woman at home who worked the most wonderful embroidery on lawn, and seeing the handkerchief and learning that it belonged to the Moor's wife, and that it was to be returned to her, she began to make a similar one before it went back. While she was doing so, the Ensign noticed that she was working near a window where she could be seen by whoever passed by on the street. So he brought the Moor and made him see her, and the latter now regarded it as certain that the most virtuous Lady was indeed an adulteress.

He arranged with the Ensign to kill her and the Corporal, and they discussed how it might be done. The Moor begged the Ensign to kill the Corporal, promising to remain eternally grateful to him. The Ensign refused to undertake such a thing, as being too difficult and dangerous, for the Corporal was as skilful as he was courageous; but after much entreaty, and being given a large sum of money, he was persuaded to say that he would tempt Fortune.

Soon after they had resolved on this, the Corporal, issuing one dark night from the house of a courtesan with whom he used to amuse himself, was accosted by the Ensign, sword in hand, who directed a blow at his legs to make him fall down; and he cut the right leg entirely through, so that the wretched man fell. The Ensign was immediately on him to finish him off, but the Corporal, who was valiant and used to blood and death, had drawn his sword, and wounded as he was he set about defending himself, while shouting in a loud voice: 'I am being murdered.'

At that the Ensign, hearing people come running ... began to flee, so as not to be caught there; then, turning back he pretended to have run up on hearing the noise. Mingling with the others, and seeing the leg cut off, he judged that if the Corporal were not already dead, he soon would die of the wound, and although he rejoiced inwardly, he outwardly grieved for the Corporal as if he had been his own brother.

[Hearing of the Corporal's death, Disdemona grieved for him; but the Moor 'put the worst possible construction' on her grief. He plotted with the Ensign to murder her; they decided to use neither poison nor the dagger, but to beat her to death with a stocking filled with sand and then pull down the ceiling to give the appearance of an accident. The Ensign hit her on the head, and Disdemona cried to the Moor for help, but he said]

'You wicked woman, you are having the reward of your infidelity.

This is how women are treated who, pretending to love their husbands, put horns on their heads.'

The wretched Lady, hearing this and feeling herself near to death (for the Ensign had given her another blow), called on Divine Justice to witness her fidelity, since earthly justice failed, and she lay still, slain by the impious Ensign ...

Next day Disdemona was buried, amid the universal mourning of the people. But God, the just observer of men's hearts, did not intend such vile wickedness to go without proper punishment. He ordained that the Moor, who had loved the Lady more than his life, on finding himself deprived of her should feel such longing that he went about like one beside himself, searching for her in every part of the house. Realizing now that the Ensign was the cause of his losing his Lady and all joy in life, he held the villain in such abhorrence that he could not bear even to see him; and if he had not been afraid of the inviolable justice of the Venetian lords, he would have slain him openly ...

[The Ensign betrayed the plot, accusing the Moor of the murder, to the Captain, who told the Venetian authorities; the Moor was arrested, tortured and condemned to exile. Eventually he was murdered by Disdemona's relatives. The Ensign was later arrested, and 'tortured so fiercely that his inner organs were ruptured'; then he was sent home, 'where he died miserably'.]

It appeared marvellous to everybody that such malignity could have been discovered in a human heart; and the fate of the unhappy Lady was lamented, with some blame for her father ... No less was the Moor blamed, who had believed too foolishly.

Critical Comments

1. THOMAS RYMER, in the seventeenth century, seemed unable to respond to the poetry and passion of *Othello,* finding the action unreasonable and the characters incredible. He concluded an essay on the play with this judgement:

> There is in this play some burlesque, some humour and ramble of comical wit, some show and some mimicry to divert the spectators; but the tragical part is none other than a bloody farce, without salt or savour.
>
> *A Short View of Tragedy,* 1693

2. SAMUEL JOHNSON, the first of Shakespeare's great editors, had the highest praise for *Othello:*

> The beauties of this play impress themselves so strongly upon the attention of the reader, that they can draw no aid from critical illustration. The fiery openness of Othello, magnanimous, artless and credulous, boundless in his confidence, ardent in his affection, inflexible in his resolution, and obdurate in his revenge; the cool malignity of Iago, silent in his resentment, subtle in his designs, and studious at once of his interest and his vengeance; the soft simplicity of Desdemona, confident of merit, and conscious of innocence, her artless perseverance in her suit, and her slowness to suspect that she can be suspected, are such proofs of Shakespeare's skill in human nature, as, I suppose, it is vain to seek in any modern writer.
>
> General Remarks on *Othello,* 1765

3. S.T. COLERIDGE, at the beginning of the nineteenth century, was impressed above all by the character of Iago, whose explanatory soliloquies he saw as

> ... the motive hunting of motiveless malignity — how awful! In itself fiendish; while yet he was allowed to bear the divine image, too fiendish for his own steady view. A being next to devil, only *not* quite devil — and this Shakespeare has attempted — and executed — without disgust, without scandal.
>
> Marginalia on *Othello*

4. A.C. BRADLEY, at the beginning of the twentieth century, was
fascinated by the character of Othello:

> Othello is, in one sense of the word, by far the most romantic
> figure among Shakespeare's heroes; and he is so partly from the
> strange life of war and adventure which he has lived from child-
> hood. He does not belong to our world, and he seems to enter it
> we do not know whence — almost as if from wonderland. There
> is something mysterious in his descent from men of royal siege; in
> his wanderings in vast deserts and among marvellous peoples; in
> his tales of magic handkerchiefs and prophetic sibyls; in the
> sudden vague glimpses we get of numberless battles and sieges in
> which he has played the hero and has born a charmed life; even in
> chance references to his baptism, his being sold to slavery, his
> sojourn in Aleppo.
>
> *Shakespearean Tragedy*, 1904

Classwork and Examinations

The works of Shakespeare are studied all over the world, and this classroom edition is being used in many different countries. Teaching methods vary from school to school and there are many different ways of examining a student's work. Some teachers and examiners expect detailed knowledge of Shakespeare's text; others ask for imaginative involvement with his characters and their situations; and there are some teachers who want their students to share in the theatrical experience of directing and performing a play. Most people use a variety of methods. This section of the book offers a few suggestions for approaches to *Othello* which could be used in schools and colleges to help with students' understanding and *enjoyment* of the play.

    A Discussion
    B Character Study
    C Activities
    D Context Questions
    E Comprehension Questions
    F Essays
    G Projects

A Discussion

Talking about the play — about the issues it raises and the characters who are involved — is one of the most rewarding and pleasurable aspects of the study of Shakespeare. It makes sense to discuss each scene as it is read, sharing impressions — and perhaps correcting misapprehensions. It can be useful to compare aspects of this play with other fictions — plays, novels, films — or with modern life.

Suggestions

A1 Iago is bitter about Cassio's 'bookish theoric', which he describes as 'Mere prattle without practice' (*1*, 1, 26). Do you think that 'paper qualifications' are more important than practical experience for many jobs?

A2 When he hears that Desdemona has eloped, Brabantio asks 'Who would be a father?' (*1*, 1, 165). What are the responsibilities of a parent? Do today's parents have more problems than those of Shakespeare's and Brabantio's time?

A3 Because Othello is black, Brabantio believes that Desdemona's love for him is 'Against all rules of nature' (*1*, 3, 101). What is your opinion of his judgement?

A4 Is Othello's jealousy a sign of his great love—or does it show a weakness in his love?

A5 Could this play be performed in modern dress? What would be the advantages and disadvantages of such a production?

B Character Study

Shakespeare is famous for his creation of characters who seem like real people. We can judge their actions and we can try to understand their thoughts and feelings—just as we criticize and try to understand the people we know. As the play progresses, we learn to like or dislike, love or hate, them—just as though they lived in *our* world. Characters can be studied *from the outside*, by observing what they do, and listening sensitively to what they say. This is the scholar's method: the scholar—or any reader—has access to the whole play, and can see the function of every character within the whole scheme of that play. Another approach works *from the inside*, taking a single character and looking at the action and the other characters from his/her point of view. This is an actor's technique when creating a single character— who can have only a partial view of what is going on—for performance; and it asks for a student's inventive imagination. The two methods— both useful in different ways—are really complementary to each other.

Suggestions

a) from 'outside' the character

B1 Write a detailed character study of

a) Roderigo
b) Cassio
c) Brabantio

B2 'I hate the Moor' (*1*, 3, 379). Examine the causes of Iago's hatred.

B3 Is Desdemona merely an innocent and passive victim?

B4 Does Emilia have a character, or simply a function?

B5   Consider Othello as an 'outsider'.

    b) from 'inside' a character

B6   In *Act 1*, Scene 3, Brabantio accused Othello of bewitching his daughter; the Moor defended himself; Desdemona supported her husband; and the Duke gave judgement and counsel. Give an account of this scene as it would be described in a personal letter (or diary, or memoir) by

    a) Brabantio   d) the Duke
    b) Othello   e) an impartial observer
    c) Desdemona   f) a witness with a strong personal opinion

B7   Roderigo must have sent letters, and perhaps even poems, expressing his love to Desdemona. Write some of these letters and poems.

B8   In *Act 3*, Scene 2 we hear that Othello has written letters to Venice. How would he have reported the success, so far, of his mission to Cyprus—and his dismissal of his lieutenant, Cassio?

B9   How would Cassio confide—either in his personal diary, or in a letter to a trusted friend in Florence—the details of his dismissal from the position of Othello's lieutenant?

B10   Write—in her personal diary—Desdemona's account of Othello's accusation in *Act 4*, Scene 2, and her reactions to it.

B11   In the character of Emilia, write to friends at home in Venice telling them about

    a) your voyage from Venice and your arrival in Cyprus.
    b) your new mistress and her husband.
    c) Iago, and his demands for Desdemona's handkerchief ('That which so often [he] did bid [you] steal'; *3, 3, 306*).

B12   Write the letters from Bianca to her girl friend—who lives some distance away—describing how you met and fell in love with lieutenant Cassio, and somehow became involved in the tragedy of Desdemona and Othello.

C   Activities

These can involve two or more students, preferably working *away from* the desk or study-table and using gesture and position ('body-language') as well as speech. They can help students to develop a sense of drama and the dramatic aspects of Shakespeare's play—which was written to be *performed*, not studied in a classroom.

Suggestions

C1 Act the play—or at least parts of it (e.g. Brabantio's accusation and Othello's defence of himself in *Act 1*, Scene 3).

C2 Perform, *using your own words*, the scene in which Iago jokes with Desdemona whilst they are waiting for Othello (*Act 2*, Scene 1); and the episode (in *Act 4*, Scene 1) where Iago and Cassio—overheard by Othello—laugh about Bianca.

C3 The Duke has called an extraordinary meeting of the senators, and a 'task force' is being sent to Cyprus (*Act 1*, Scene 3). This will be given full coverage by all the media—newspapers, radio, and television. Research the 'background' of the Turkish problem, and assess the threat to Venice if Cyprus is invaded. What can be found out about Othello, the General chosen to lead the task force? Is anything known about the second-in-command, a 'foreigner' from Florence? Was there no Venetian who could do this job? An unexpected development arises when senator Brabantio reveals the secret marriage of his daughter and accuses the General of seducing her. How will the media react to this scandal?

C4 Devise additional scenes in which

a) Iago persuades Emilia to speak to Desdemona and 'move for Cassio' (2, 3, 274).
b) Othello tells Desdemona why he has dismissed Cassio. ('The general and his wife are talking of it' — 3, 1, 42).
c) Lodovico, returned home from Cyprus, tells his friends what he has seen ('this would not be believed in Venice' — 4, 1, 238).
d) Othello talks to Lodovico as he escorts him to his lodgings (''twill do me good to walk' — 4, 3, 2).

C5 Arrange the trial—with full media coverage—of Iago. Thoroughly investigate the lives of his chief victims—and don't forget Roderigo! How was Iago able to win the trust of so many people?

D Context Questions

In written examinations, these questions present you with short passages from the play, and ask you to explain them. They are intended to test your knowledge of the play and your understanding of its words. Usually you have to make a choice of passages: there may be five on the paper, and you are asked to choose three. Be very sure that you know exactly how many passages you must choose. Study the ones offered to you, and select those you feel most certain of. Make your answers accurate and concise—don't waste time writing more than the examiner is asking for.

D1   Believe me, I had rather have lost my purse
Full of crusadoes; and, but my noble Moor
Is true of mind, and made of no such baseness
As jealous creatures are, it were enough
To put him to ill-thinking.

    (i) Who speaks these words, and to whom are they spoken?
    (ii) Who is the 'noble Moor' of whom the speaker is so confident?
    (iii) Is the speaker's confidence well placed?
    (iv) What is the 'ill-thinking' that arises?

D2   Sir, she can turn, and turn, and yet go on,
And turn again. And she can weep, sir, weep.
And she's obedient; as you say, obedient,
Very obedient—proceed you in your tears—
Concerning this, sir—O, well-painted passion!—

    (i) Who is the speaker, and to whom is he speaking?
    (ii) Who is 'she'?
    (iii) What has the speaker just done?

D3   For do but stand upon the banning shore,
The chidden billow seems to pelt the clouds,
The wind-shaked surge, with high and monstrous main,
Seems to cast water on the burning Bear
And quench the guards of th'ever-fixèd Pole.

    (i) Who speaks these lines, and who is listening?
    (ii) What is the speaker describing?
    (iii) For whom are they waiting?

E   Comprehension Questions

These also present passages from the play and ask questions about them, and again you often have a choice of passages. But the extracts are much longer than those presented as context questions. A detailed knowledge of the language of the play is asked for here, and you must be able to express unusual or archaic phrases in your own words; you may also be asked to comment critically on the effectiveness of Shakespeare's language.

E1 *Brabantio*
For I'll refer me to all things of sense,
If she in chains of magic were not bound,
Whether a maid, so tender, fair, and happy,
So opposite to marriage that she shunned
The wealthy curlèd darlings of our nation,   5
Would ever have—t'incur a general mock —
Run from her guardage to the sooty bosom
Of such a thing as thou: to fear, not to delight.
Judge me the world, if 'tis not gross in sense
That thou hast practised on her with foul charms,   10
Abused her delicate youth with drugs or minerals
That weakens motion.

  (i) Give the precise context of Brabantio's speech.
 (ii) What is the meaning of 'all things of sense' (line 1); 'a general mock' (line 6); 'guardage' (line 7); 'sooty bosom' (line 7).
(iii) Express in your own words the meaning of lines 4–5 ('So opposite . . . nation'); and lines 9–12 ('Judge me . . . motion').
(iv) Comment on Brabantio's use of language in this speech.

E2 *Iago*
Mark me with what violence she first loved the Moor, but for bragging and telling her fantastical lies. And will she love him still for prating? Let not thy discreet heart think it. Her eye must be fed. And what delight shall she have to look on the devil? When the blood is made dull with   5
the act of sport, there should be, again to inflame it and give satiety a fresh appetite, loveliness in favour, sympathy in years, manners and beauties: all which the Moor is defective in. Now for want of these required conveniences, her delicate tenderness will find itself   10
abused, begin to heave the gorge, disrelish and abhor the Moor. Very nature will instruct her in it and compel her to some second choice.

(i) Give the exact context of this passage, identifying both the speaker and the person spoken to.
(ii) Give the meaning of 'still' (line 3); 'prating' (line 3); 'discreet' (line 3); 'heave the gorge' (line 11).
(iii) Express in your own words the meaning of lines 5–8 ('When . . . beauties').
(iv) Comment on the imagery of these lines.

E3   *Othello*
That handkerchief
Did an Egyptian to my mother give:
She was a charmer and could also read
The thoughts of people. She told her, while she kept it,
'Twould make her amiable and subdue my father   5
Entirely to her love; but if she lost it
Or made a gift of it, my father's eye
Should hold her loathèd, and his spirits should hunt
After new fancies. She, dying, gave it to me,
And bid me, when my fate would have me wive,   10
To give it her. I did so; and take heed on't:
Make it a darling like your precious eye.
To lose or give't away were such perdition
As nothing else could match.
Desdemona
                                        Is't possible?
Othello
'Tis true: there's magic in the web of it.   15

(i) What has happened to the 'handkerchief' that Othello is describing here? Where will it next be seen?
(ii) Express in your own words the meaning of lines 4–6 ('She told her . . . her love'); and line 12 ('Make . . . eye').
(iii) Explain what is meant by 'a charmer' (line 3); 'hold her loathèd' (line 8); 'wive' (line 10); 'perdition' (line 13).
(iv) What do these lines show of Othello's character?

F   Essays

These will usually give you a specific topic to discuss, or perhaps a question that must be answered, in writing, *with a reasoned argument*. They *never* want you to tell the story of the play—so don't! Your examiner—or teacher—has read the play and does not need to be reminded of it. Relevant quotations will always help you to make your points more strongly.

F1   The Italian story on which *Othello* is based says that the characters sailed to Cyprus on 'a sea of the utmost tranquillity'. Why do you think that Shakespeare invented the tempestuous storm described in *Act 2*, Scene 2?

F2   In the source narrative, the Ensign's motive is frustrated lust, whereas in the play Iago seems to be driven by thwarted ambition; which of these do you find the more convincing motive for such villainy?

F3   What other points of difference do you find between the play and its source?

F4   Examine the different ways in which Iago manipulates the other characters; to what extent is he the 'stage-manager' of the play?

F5   What methods does Shakespeare use for breaking the tension?

G   Projects

In some schools, students are asked to do more 'free-ranging' work, which takes them outside the text—but which should always be relevant to the play. Such Projects may demand skills other than reading and writing: design and artwork, for instance, may be involved. Sometimes a 'portfolio' of work is assembled over a considerable period of time; and this can be presented to the examiner as part of the student's work for assessment.

The availability of resources will, obviously, do much to determine the nature of the Projects; but this is something that only the local teachers will understand. However, there is always help to be found in libraries, museums, and art galleries.

Suggestions

G1   Venice.

G2   Colour Prejudice.

G3   The Outsider.

G4   Famous Performances.

G5   Costumes.

Background

England c. *1604*

When Shakespeare was writing *Othello*, most people believed that the sun went round the earth. They were taught that this was a divinely ordered scheme of things, and that—in England—God had instituted a Church and ordained a Monarchy for the right government of the land and the populace.

'The past is a foreign country; they do things differently there.'

L.P. Hartley

Government

For most of Shakespeare's life, the reigning monarch of England was Queen Elizabeth I; when she died, she was succeeded by King James I. He was also king of Scotland (James VI), and the two kingdoms were united in 1603 by his accession to the English throne. With his counsellors and ministers, James governed the nation (population less than six million) from London, although not more than half a million people inhabited the capital city. In the rest of the country, law and order were maintained by the land-owners and enforced by their deputies. The average man had no vote—and his wife had no rights at all.

Religion

At this time, England was a Christian country. All children were baptized, soon after they were born, into the Church of England; they were taught the essentials of the Christian faith, and instructed in their duty to God and to humankind. Marriages were performed, and funerals conducted, only by the licensed clergy and in accordance with the Church's rites and ceremonies. Attendance at divine service was compulsory; absences (without good—medical—reason) could be punished by fines. By such means, the authorities were able to keep some check on the populace—recording births, marriages, and deaths; being alert to any religious nonconformity, which could be politically dangerous; and ensuring a minimum of orthodox instruction through the official 'Homilies' which were regularly preached from the pulpits of all parish churches throughout the realm. Following Henry VIII's break away from the Church of Rome, all people in England were able to hear the church services *in their own language*. The Book of Common Prayer was used in every church, and an English translation of the Bible was read aloud in public. The Christian religion had never been so well taught before!

Education

School education reinforced the Church's teaching. From the age of four, boys might attend the 'petty school' (French '*petite école*') to learn the rudiments of reading and writing along with a few prayers; some schools also included work with numbers. At the age of seven, the boy was ready for the grammar school (if his father was willing and able to pay the fees). Here, a thorough grounding in Latin grammar was followed by translation work and the study of Roman authors, paying attention as much to style as to matter. The arts of fine writing were thus inculcated from early youth. A very few students proceeded to university; these were either clever scholarship boys, or else the sons of noblemen.

Girls stayed at home, and acquired domestic and social skills—cooking, sewing, perhaps even music. The lucky ones might learn to read and write.

Language

At the start of the sixteenth century the English had a very poor opinion of their own language: there was little serious writing in English, and hardly any literature. Latin was the language of international scholarship, and Englishmen admired the eloquence of the Romans. They made many translations, and in this way they extended the resources of their own language, increasing its vocabulary and stretching its grammatical structures. French, Italian, and Spanish works were also translated, and—for the first time—there were English versions of the Bible. By the end of the century, English was a language to be proud of: it was rich in synonyms, capable of infinite variety and subtlety, and ready for all kinds of word-play—especially the *puns*, for which Shakespeare's English is renowned.

Drama

The great art-form of the Elizabethan and Jacobean age was its drama. The Elizabethans inherited a tradition of play-acting from the Middle

Ages, and they reinforced this by reading and translating the Roman playwrights. At the beginning of the sixteenth century, plays were performed by groups of actors, all-male companies (boys acted the female roles) who travelled from town to town, setting up their stages in open places (such as inn-yards) or, with the permission of the owner, in the hall of some noble house. The touring companies continued, in the provinces, into the seventeenth century; but in London, in 1576, a new building was erected for the performance of plays. This was the Theatre, the first purpose-built playhouse in England. Other playhouses followed—including the Globe, where most of Shakespeare's plays were performed. The English drama reached new heights of eloquence.

There were those who disapproved, of course. The theatres, which brought large crowds together, could encourage the spread of disease—and dangerous ideas. During the summer, when the plague was at its worst, the playhouses were closed. A constant censorship was imposed, more or less severe at different times. The Puritan faction tried to close down the theatres, but—partly because there was royal favour for the drama, and partly because the buildings were outside the city limits—they did not succeed until 1642.

Theatre

From contemporary comments and sketches—most particularly a drawing by a Dutch visitor, Johannes de Witt—it is possible to form some idea of the typical Elizabethan playhouse for which most of Shakespeare's plays were written. Hexagonal in shape, it had three roofed galleries encircling an open courtyard. The plain, high stage projected into the yard, where it was surrounded by the audience of standing 'groundlings'. At the back were two doors for the actors' entrances and exits; and above these doors was a balcony—useful for a musicians' gallery or for the acting of scenes 'above'. Over the stage was a thatched roof, supported on two pillars, forming a canopy—which seems to have been painted with the sun, moon, and stars for the 'heavens'.

Underneath was space (concealed by curtaining) which could be used by characters ascending and descending through a trapdoor in the stage. Costumes and properties were kept backstage, in the 'tiring house'. The actors dressed lavishly, often wearing the secondhand clothes bestowed by rich patrons. Stage properties were important for defining a location, but the dramatist's own words were needed to explain the time of day, since all performances took place in the early afternoon.

Suggested Further Reading

Bayley, John, 'Love and Identity: *Othello*' in *The Characters of Love*, (1962).

Gardner, Helen, *The Noble Moor*, (Proceedings of the British Academy, 1955).

Jones, Eldred, *Othello's Countrymen: the African in English Renaissance Drama*, (Oxford University Press, 1965).

Knight, G. Wilson, 'The Othello Music' in *The Wheel of Fire*, (Methuen, 1930).

Leavis, F.R., 'Diabolic Intellect and the Noble Hero' in *The Common Pursuit*, (Chatto & Windus, 1952).

Muir, Kenneth, *The Sources of Shakespeare's Plays*, (London, 1977).

Some of these, with other excellent essays, are published in *Shakespeare: 'Othello'*, a Casebook edited by John Wain (Macmillan, 1971).

Background Reading

Blake, N.F., *Shakespeare's Language: an Introduction*, (Methuen, 1983).

Muir, K., and Schoenbaum, S., *A New Companion to Shakespeare Studies*, (Cambridge, 1971).

Schoenbaum, S., *William Shakespeare: A Documentary Life*, (Oxford, 1975).

Thomson, Peter, *Shakespeare's Theatre*, (Routledge and Kegan Paul, 1983).

William Shakespeare, 1564-1616

Elizabeth I was Queen of England when Shakespeare was born in 1564. He was the son of a tradesman who made and sold gloves in the small town of Stratford-upon-Avon, and he was educated at the grammar school in that town. Shakespeare did not go to university when he left school, but worked, perhaps in his father's business. When he was eighteen he married Anne Hathaway, who became the mother of his daughter, Susanna, in 1583, and of twins in 1585.

There is nothing exciting, or even unusual, in this story; and from 1585 until 1592 there are no documents that can tell us anything at all about Shakespeare. But we have learned that in 1592 he was known in London, and that he had become both an actor and a playwright.

We do not know when Shakespeare wrote his first play, and indeed we are not sure of the order in which he wrote his works. If you look on page 144 at the list of his writings and their approximate dates, you will see how he started by writing plays on subjects taken from the history of England. No doubt this was partly because he was always an intensely patriotic man—but he was also a very shrewd business man. He could see that the theatre audiences enjoyed being shown their own history, and it was certain that he would make a profit from this kind of drama.

The plays in the next group are mainly comedies, with romantic love stories of young people who fall in love with one another and, at the end of the play, marry and live happily ever after. *Twelfth Night* is the last of these.

At the end of the sixteenth century the happiness disappears, and Shakespeare's plays become melancholy, bitter, and tragic. This change may have been caused by some sadness in the writer's life (one of his twins died in 1596). Shakespeare, however, was not the only writer whose works at this time were very serious. The whole of England was facing a crisis. Queen Elizabeth I was growing old. She was greatly loved, and the people were sad to think she must soon die; they were also afraid, for the Queen had never married, and so there was no child to succeed her.

When James I came to the throne in 1603, Shakespeare continued to write serious drama—the great tragedies and the plays based on Roman history (such as *Julius Caesar*) for which he is most famous.

Finally, before he retired from the theatre, he wrote another set of comedies. These all have the same theme: they tell of happiness which is lost, and then found again.

Shakespeare returned from London to Stratford, his home town. He was rich and successful, and he owned one of the biggest houses in the town. He died in 1616. Although several of his plays were published separately, most of them were not printed until 1623, in a collection known as 'the First Folio'.

Shakespeare also wrote two long poems, and a collection of sonnets. The sonnets describe two love-affairs, but we do not know who the lovers were. Although there are many public documents concerned with his career as a writer and a businessman, Shakespeare has hidden his personal life from us. A nineteenth-century poet, Matthew Arnold, addressed Shakespeare in a poem and wrote 'We ask and ask—Thou smilest and art still'.

There is not even a trustworthy portrait of the world's greatest dramatist.

Approximate order of composition of Shakespeare's works

Period	Comedies	History plays	Tragedies	Poems
I 1594	Comedy of Errors Taming of the Shrew Two Gentlemen of Verona Love's Labour's Lost	Henry VI, part 1 Henry VI, part 2 Henry VI, part 3 Richard III King John	Titus Andronicus	 Venus and Adonis Rape of Lucrece
II 1599	Midsummer Night's Dream Merchant of Venice Merry Wives of Windsor Much Ado About Nothing As You Like it	Richard II Henry IV, part 1 Henry IV, part 2 Henry V	Romeo and Juliet	Sonnets
III 1608	Twelfth Night Troilus and Cressida Measure for Measure All's Well That Ends Well		Julius Caesar Hamlet Othello Timon of Athens King Lear Macbeth Antony and Cleopatra Coriolanus	
IV 1613	Pericles Cymbeline The Winter's Tale The Tempest	 Henry VIII		